VIVA MEZCAL

Sipping, Mixing & Other Adventures with Mexico's Original Handcrafted Spirit

Lindsey Moore
& Jennifer Boudinot

Bluestreak
BOOKS

Para todo mal, mezcal;
para todo bien, también.

‹ ‹ ‹ ‹ ‹

For everything bad, mezcal;
and also, for everything good.

—Mexican proverb

ACKNOWLEDGMENTS

Thank you to everyone who contributed cocktail recipes, provided photographs or information, and otherwise supported us in making this book, including: Meredith Sheehy, Jeff Burfield, and everyone at La Loba Cantina; Michael Brooker, Dylan March, Herminio Torres, Heather Rodino, Will Aaron, Jordan Brower, José María Dondé Rangel and Panorama Mezcal, Harris Tooley, Brian Evans, Jen Marshall, Camille Austin, Jesús Díaz, Carlos Abeyta, Gabriela Martinez Benecke, Mark Gore, Lynne Yeamans, Patrice Kaplan, Karen Matsu Greenberg and Christopher Navratil.

Bluestreak Books is an imprint of Weldon Owen,
a Bonnier Publishing USA company
www.bonnierpublishingusa.com

ISBN 978-1-68188-330-4

Packaged by Hourglass Press
Photos: Mark A. Gore
Cover and interior design: Patrice Kaplan

First Printed in 2018
10 9 8 7 6 5 4 3 2

Printed in Turkey by Elma Basim

Contents

Introduction

Mezcal is a dream, lit by a fire, where you're surrounded by comrades whose faces you don't need to see to know they're friends. A burst of laughter seems imminent. Something important is happening even though, really, nothing is happening. The universe makes sense even if the "how" or the "why" doesn't. You know you're in a dream though you don't feel the need to wake up.

When I first started drinking mezcal, in a Brooklyn cantina where my friend Lindsey was working behind the bar, I thought it was just another liquor—a fancy version of tequila that made margaritas taste better. Like most casual drinkers, all I had to say about it was "I like it, it's smoky." Thankfully, Lindsey didn't roll her eyes in frustration at this comment. Instead, she

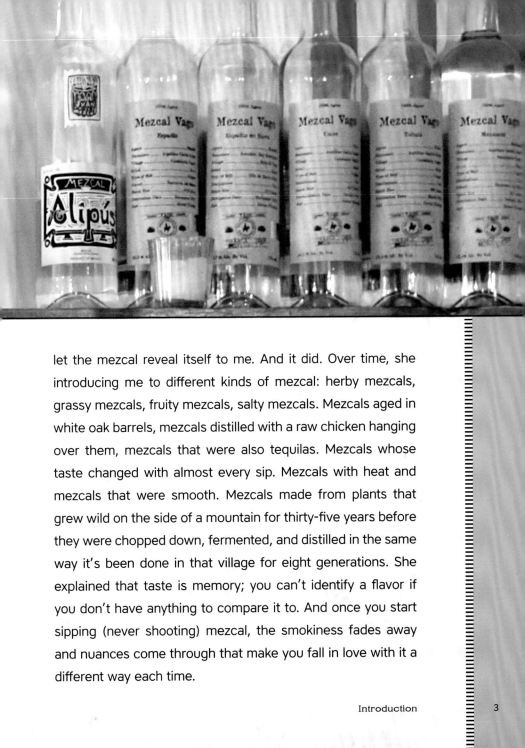

let the mezcal reveal itself to me. And it did. Over time, she introducing me to different kinds of mezcal: herby mezcals, grassy mezcals, fruity mezcals, salty mezcals. Mezcals aged in white oak barrels, mezcals distilled with a raw chicken hanging over them, mezcals that were also tequilas. Mezcals whose taste changed with almost every sip. Mezcals with heat and mezcals that were smooth. Mezcals made from plants that grew wild on the side of a mountain for thirty-five years before they were chopped down, fermented, and distilled in the same way it's been done in that village for eight generations. She explained that taste is memory; you can't identify a flavor if you don't have anything to compare it to. And once you start sipping (never shooting) mezcal, the smokiness fades away and nuances come through that make you fall in love with it a different way each time.

In Oaxaca, Mexico (where most mezcal is from), in small Brooklyn cantinas, and in mezcalerías (mezcal bars) throughout the world, mezcal is about more than getting drunk. It's a reason to get together with loved ones away from the daily grind and to experience something—like a card or dice game among an old group of friends who have been playing together so long the rules remain unspoken because everyone knows them by heart. As Ulises Torrentera, one of the grandfathers of mezcal, wrote in the definitive history of mezcal, *Mezcalaria*:

> Take my advice: if your partner cheats on you, drink mezcal; even if you only have your suspicions, drink mezcal. If you are unfaithful, drink mezcal; if you are monogamous, drink mezcal! If you have doubts about something, drink mezcal; and if you are absolutely confident about everything, drink mezcal. At any time and under any conditions, always drink mezcal. As the saying goes, *For everything bad, mezcal; and also, for everything good.*

Inside this book, a loving ode to our favorite spirit, you'll find information on how mezcal is made and what to look for when buying it, the different varieties and what they taste like, how to sip mezcal and expand your palate, how to create perfectly balanced cocktails with this unique base spirit, and other fun tidbits. Lindsey and I can't pretend to unleash the dreamlike power that is mezcal, but we hope to be helpful guides on your journey of discovering mezcal for yourself.

—*Jennifer Boudinot*

What Is Mezcal?

Besides being a magical elixir, mezcal is a distillate of the agave plant. ("Distillate" is a fancy word for a "liquid product condensed from vapor"). Like French champagne or cognac, the term *mezcal* is regulated, and real mezcals can only be made from agave grown in Oaxaca or certain other Mexican states.

According to Torrentera's *Mezcalaria*, the agave plant [family Agavaceae. Genus *Agave*: numerous species] has been around forever—fossils of agave leaves have been found in the stomachs of ancient humans who lived a mind-blowing *nine thousand* years ago—and mezcal itself has been around at least since the sixteenth century. In Mexico, the tradition of making mezcal has been passed down for countless generations.

Most villages have a *mezcalero* (mezcal maker) with a small staff, in the same way they might have a butcher or baker, and different varieties of mezcal have been developed based on the types of agave that grow nearby. Even more taste variations have been introduced through the unique way each *mezcalero* roasts, ferments, and distills the ancient spirit.

Defining "Legal" Mezcal

Mezcal has an Appellation of Origin (AO), which it was granted in 1995 by the World Intellectual Property Organization (WIPO), the UN agency that designates such things. This means that like cognac, champagne, and tequila, you can only call your agave-based spirit mezcal if it's made in Oaxaca or eight other Mexican states (Durango, Guanajuato, Guerrero, San Luis Potosí, Tamaulipas, Zacatecas, Michoacan, and the recently approved Puebla).

Mexico also has its own Denominación de Origen (DO) standards, and that's where things start to get tricky. Mexico's laws regulating the production, naming and classification of mezcal change continually. Some of these regulations are good ones—like the requirement that mezcal must be bottled at the distillery and that to get the highest ("Type I") ranking mezcal has to be made with 100 percent agave. Other regulations seem arbitrary, such as the fact that certain types of traditional stills are restricted for the "ancestral" classification while modern agave-crushing methods are not. There are Mexican states that have a long history of producing mezcal that were left off the list of states that could legally put the word on their bottles. Other rules seem to put small producers at a disadvantage while some regulations actually downgraded what could be called "mezcal" by including products that have artificial sweeteners and those that are produced using industrial methods—and none of the regulations address sustainability issues.

If you really want to get into the nitty-gritty of these laws, search "Mexican mezcal regulations" online and read what some excellent blogs have to say on the subject. But as far as what mezcal you should or shouldn't be drinking, the best thing to do is simply ask a knowledgeable bartender or liquor store clerk, rather than looking to the government (any government). —JB

Although mezcal from the Agave tequilana plant (aka tequila)* became popular much earlier, other mezcals weren't commercially produced and exported until around twenty-five to thirty years ago, when the company Del Maguey started importing them into the US. Run by a guy named Ron Cooper (who was originally a successful visual artist), Del Maguey began when Cooper and some of his road trip buds stumbled upon an eight-day, mezcal-fueled wedding party in Teotitlán del Valle, a Zapotec village in Oaxaca. He fell in love with mezcal and everything that goes with it (like so many of us do), but when he tried to bring a jug of it back to the United States, it was confiscated at the border. Not one to be stopped, he's been importing mezcal from that very village almost ever since.

When mezcal first found me, it was 2013 and I had just moved to New York from Austin, Texas. I was already familiar with the mysterious spirit—it was featured in some of the cocktails at the bar I had worked at in Austin, and before that I had worked at a tequila bar (it *was* Texas, after all). But when I came to New York, I began to fall in love with mezcal as a cocktail spirit, experimenting with it in classic cocktails and finding that mezcal worked in every single one— whether the base spirit had originally been whiskey, vodka, rum, or even gin. I also met my friend Herminio, a regular at the Brooklyn

---

*Yes, all tequilas are mezcals. But not all mezcals are tequila! See page 15 for more info.

In 2005 Mexico established an organization to set industry standards for mezcal and to certify producers, and in the past five to seven years, mezcal has boomed. Now, liquor companies and aficionados like Cooper are tapping *mezcaleros* from all over the region to export their own unique mezcals. (See page 104 for more on how this is affecting the region and the agave plant itself.) Cooper loves the saying, "You don't find mezcal. Mezcal finds you." It's now finding people all over the world. Mezcalerías are popping up in pretty much every major city in Mexico and the US, as well as in places as far-flung as Paris, Milan, Copenhagen, Tokyo, Hong Kong, and Sydney—where it's almost as popular as it is in the US (although much more expensive).

dive where I worked. Herminio, who works for the mezcal company Ilegal, introduced me to mezcals made from different agave varietals, and soon I drank a mezcal made from tobalá that changed my life. I had fallen hard for mezcal. A few years later, I was introducing people to mezcal every day as head bartender at a mezcalería, La Loba Cantina, and I even traveled to Oaxaca to visit *palenques*, the humble distilleries where mezcal is made.

Mezcal is my favorite spirit for a number of reasons. First, there's the taste: unlike a spirit such as whiskey, which takes most of its flavor from the barrels it's aged in, mezcal's flavor comes largely from the agave itself. Agave plants—many of which grow wild in Mexico—can come in all sorts of shapes and sizes, giving mezcal a natural variety of taste before it even gets put in the still. Mezcal is also made through an artisanal process rather than being produced in a factory. It's organic and has no additives. It's just a roasted plant, fermented in bottles—a booze salad, if you will. That means that not only is it all-natural, but it won't give you a hangover, unless you really overdo it.

The important thing to remember is that—while we've tried to give you a good overview of what mezcal is all about—you don't have to know everything about it to enjoy it. For me, mezcal has energetic properties—it brings an infectious, happy spirit to the bar and I love serving it to people. I hope this book brings more mezcal love into your life. *Salud!*

—*Lindsey Moore*

Mezcal Types

There are many different types of mezcal, each with its own characteristics and flavor profile. However, because mezcal draws so much of its flavor from the agave plant itself, over the years, the taste of various varietials of mezcals will change over time. As the agave plants are grown in different territories, farmed rather than harvested in the wild, and exposed to different environmental elements, their characteristics will slowly change. Use these tasting notes as a jumping off point for your journey.

◆ ◆ ◆ ◆ ◆

Young vs. Aged

Joven

Most mezcal is *joven* ("HO-vin"), or unaged. Joven, meaning "young," is the best way to experience all of the nuanced flavors of agave. (Some mezcal purists even believe that aging mezcal ruins it.) You'll see joven mezcal in most of our cocktail recipes. On tequila bottles, you'll see the word "blanco" (white) or "plata" (silver) instead of "joven."

Reposado

Although not common, aged mezcals are becoming more popular, especially as mezcal companies try to appeal to people more accustomed to the flavors of whiskey and rum. We think aged mezcals, particularly reposados ("ray-poe-SAH-dos"), can make a good gateway drug for newbie mezcal drinkers, because the wood chills out the characteristic smoky taste of joven mezcal, but it doesn't completely wash out its nuances. *Reposado* means "rested"—these mezcals are usually aged in oak barrels for up to a year. We recommend Ilegal's offering, which brings to mind hints of vanilla and orange zest and even a subtle taste of pumpkin pie.

Añejo

Añejo ("un-YAY-ho") means "old" or "aged," and like reposado mezcals, añejo mezcals are aged in oak (oftentimes charred) barrels, but for up to three years. Again, the aging process and the flavors picked up from the oak tend to mask the flavors of the agave, sometimes making it taste like a completely different spirit. However, a skilled mezcalero can make a great añejo. Ilegal, once again, is a leader in this space, producing a terrific añejo that's aged thirteen months and has hints of maple and clove, though it still tastes like agave.

◈ ◈ ◈ ◈ ◈

Agave Varietals

Unique among liquors with most of its flavor coming from the plant rather than from aging (like whiskey) or other infusions (like gin), agave covers the ground in much of Mexico. Most mezcals are made from the espadín varietal of mezcal, but in Mexico, more than fifty different types of agave are used to make mezcal, and more than a dozen of these can be found in the US. The type of agave used greatly impacts the flavor of the spirit, so trying more exotic kinds of mezcal can lead the discovery of entirely new tastes.*

If you're a wine drinker you may remember that in the first few months you started drinking wine, you probably couldn't tell the difference between a pinot noir and a cabernet sauvignon. In the same way, when you first drink different mezcals, they will simply taste like mezcal. Once you become more experienced with mescal, you'll start to notice the different characteristics of the various types of agave (and you might even fall in love). These types are organized into varietals and subvarietals, based on the scientific name of the agave. Here are some you should know, listed by their most common name. Once you've mastered these, start exploring others!

Espadín

About 80 percent of all mezcals are made from the espadín subvarietal of *Agave angustifolia*. That's because espadín ("ess-pa-DEEN") takes only eight years to mature (compared to more than a decade, as with some other varieties), has a high sugar content (so it doesn't take long to ferment), and is so hardy that it's not only easy to grow yourself, but grows wild through much of the mezcal-producing regions of Mexico. Also, it's delicious.

---

*Check out page 82 for more on how agave is produced and page 104 for info on the long-term sustainability of agave plants.

A pure representation of roasted agave, espadín starts off with the taste of roasted red pepper and then brightens up with notes of citrus and greenery. If you use agave nectar as a sweetener, you'll notice they smell very similar! Espadín is the best mezcal to start off with if you're new to the spirit. Begin with some mezcal joven by Ilegal, then try out some Del Maguey Chichicapa (as fun to say as it is to drink). Once you can pick out the flavors in these, try sipping try sipping Fidencio's espadín offering—one of our favorites.

Pechuga and Other Infused Mezcals

Infused mezcals are deliciously complex. Dried fruit, corn, herbs, or other ingredients are added to the still during distillation to impart specific flavor characteristics to the mezcal. A tobalá mezcal called +9 Botanicals from Pierde Almas adds botanicals, including juniper berry. Pierde Almas calls it a "New World Gin," and notes on their website, "Instead of the juniper standing out front in the role of lonely soloist, it truly blends with a complex chorus of spices." Mezcal Vago's Elote, is a sweet, full mezcal that has roasted corn added after the second distillation; it's then rested a few days before being distilled a third time.

One of the most original types of infused mezcal is pechuga, available in the US from Del Maguey and Fidencio, among other brands. *Pechuga* means "breast" in Spanish—as in chicken breast. Pechuga mezcal is made by hanging a raw chicken (or even rabbit) breast over the still while the agave is roasting, so that the mezcal vapors run through the meat and are then infused back into the mezcal itself. Seasonal fruits and nuts are also thrown into the still, giving pechuga a "meat, yet sweet" flavor.

Tobalá

Tobalá is a floral, mineral varietal. A rare agave that grows at a higher elevation (and cooler climate) than most agaves, it's also one of the smallest. While the *piña* (the part of the agave used to make mezcal) of an espadín agave is so big it takes three people to roll it, tobalá ("toe-ball-AH") is only about the size of a basketball, even at its biggest. Because tobalá grows wild on the sides of mountains and can take up to twenty-five years to mature, it's harder to come by and much more prized than other kinds of mezcal.

Mezcal experts worry that the popularity of tobalá mezcal will lead to the plant becoming endangered, so if you have an opportunity to try this unique spirit now, take it. Its taste and smell of freshly cut flowers will knock you over (even though it somehow remains delicate), and its earthiness with a hint of salt reminds you that it was grown on the side of a cliff. Try the tobalá by Mezcal Vago, whose labels tell you everything, down to the mezcalero's name, what village he's from, and how hard he grinds the agave. Vago's commitment to mezcal is so strong that the label itself is made of *bagaso*, the burned agave leaves that are left after roasting.

Karwinski (Including Tobasiche and Barril)

Unlike the other agaves in this section, which are technically subvarietals of various agave species, karwinski is a whole varietal unto itself, with many well-known subvarietals including cuixe, barril, and especially tobasiche. Karwinski is a wild agave that you'll see everywhere if you spend time in the mezcal-producing regions of

Mexico. Unlike most agaves that are short and squat (essentially growing out before they grow up), the tall, skinny agave karwinski plant grows up and then out, eventually looking almost like a palm tree. It takes twelve to thirteen years to fully mature and produces a mezcal that's mineral and floral with a hint of botanicals. As for brands, try Koch's rich and fruity Mezcal Barril or Rey Campero's Madre-Cuishe, which has hints of vanilla. Koch also makes a wonderful tobasiche, as does Bozal. And if you happen to find yourself in Oaxaca, get your hands on a vibrant, lively karwinski verde, which is practically impossible to find in the US.

Arroqueño

Arroqueño ("arr-oh-CANE-yo") stands out for its richness and sweetness. Not for beginners, this varietal makes a hot, complex mezcal with notes of roasted chile peppers, dark chocolate, and over-ripened blackberries and raspberries. Somewhat rare, arroqueño can be either wild or cultivated (or a combination of both). It is also a bit unpredictable in that the number of years it takes to flower (mature) varies. Try Los Siete Misterios's offering.

Cupreata

Also called papalome or papalometl, cupreata ("coo-pray-OTT-a") is known for its strong vegetal notes. Usually found in the wild but sometimes grown on farms, cupreatas take seven to ten years to reach maturity. Cupreata distillates have a seemingly endless number of flavor undertones, ranging from cucumber and celery to mushrooms, black olives, and leather. Del Maguey's Wild Papalometl is a nice-'n'-meaty mezcal from Oaxaca with savory hints of leather and olive brine. Del Maguey also has an interesting, floral cupreata from the new mezcal-producing state of Puebla (called Mezcal de Puebla). Meanwhile, Mezcales de Leyenda has a cupreata from Guerro (also named after the state it's from). It's light and vegetal, with earthy notes and a hint of papaya.

Tequila

Tequila is a mezcal made from the blue weber agave plant. Yep, that's right—tequila is a type of mezcal. Good tequila (see next page) tastes fresh and ripe with a touch of sweetness, but its most notable difference from other mezcals (besides its popularity in the US) is the way it's made. After being harvested, the blue weber agaves are roasted in clay ovens, away from the agave being distilled. With other mezcals, the agaves are roasted in the open air, in close proximity to the distilling mezcal. This allows the distillate to pick up the smoky smell and taste from the air, giving it its characteristic quality. Tequila is originally from the Mexican state of Jalisco (home of the city of Tequila), and legally, spirits labeled "tequila" can only come from Jalisco or a small handful of nearby regions. Stay away from any tequila that doesn't say "100 percent blue agave" somewhere on it. Tequila Ocho and Siembra Valles (which also makes a great mezcal) are excellent choices.

Tequila vs. Mezcal: What's the Difference?

If you're talking about pure, artisanal spirits, there are only two real differences between tequila and mezcal: first, tequila is made solely from blue weber agave, while mezcal is made from numerous other agave varietals, and second, the process for making tequila varies somewhat from traditional mezcal, so it doesn't usually taste as smoky. But thanks to tequila's longstanding popularity in the US and the proliferation of large, corporate tequila brands, the difference between what's available in the United States as "tequila" vs. what's available as "mezcal" has gotten more complicated.

Let's go back to 1888. Like just about everywhere in Mexico, Jalisco had its own mezcal based on the kind of agave common to the region—in this case, the *agave tequilana*, or blue weber. But unlike elsewhere in Mexico, Jalisco had a central location (Tequila) where mezcal producers from rural areas had moved their production to take advantage of what the Mexican government and President Porfirio Díaz had promised would be a big boom in mezcal production and export. At the government's urging, they modernized their manufacturing methods and started using clay ovens, which cut agave roasting time in half and also removed it's traditional smoky flavor. In 1888, Jalisco's new railway was completed, and large-scale exportation of mezcal from Tequila, later marketed as a spirit called "tequila," began.

In 1893, Cenobio Sauza brought tequila, which he called *vino mescal*, to the World's Fair in Chicago, where it won widespread recognition and spread like wildfire throughout the United States—you may have had Sauza tequila yourself at some point. The tequila industry boomed during Prohibition, when it was smuggled north over the border; its popularity surged again during World War II, when importing whiskey from Europe became difficult. By the 1960s, as Americans embraced margaritas and tequila sunrises, agave was becoming scarce in Jalisco, so the Mexican government passed regulations allowing tequila to be made with plants other than agave, like corn. It also allowed flavorings and dyes to be added. That's right, "gold" tequila isn't aged; it just has dye added. (For real aged tequila, look for a 100 percent agave brand with the word "reposado" or "añejo" on the bottle.)

Although in the 1990s the tequila company Patrón began a return to 100 percent–agave tequila and many quality brands (large and small) have followed, when you visit a liquor store or dive bar, most of what you'll find is the industrialized bad stuff—further muddling the distinction between what's known as "tequila" and what's known as "mezcal," which has higher purity standards. When buying or ordering tequila, make sure to check the label for that "100," or just stick with mezcal, which is always 100 percent good stuff.

Even More Agave Varietals

There are many more varietals of agave that are made into mezcal: mexicano, a relative of espadín; tepeztate, taking twenty-five to thirty years to grow; coyote, which grows high in the mountains and can cost up to $170 a bottle; and plenty of others that are hard to find in the US. Also worth checking out are *ensambles*, where a mezcalaro expertly blends together several different varietals of agave. For instance, Bozal has an espadín, barril, and mexicano *ensamble* that we drank a lot while writing this book. Try these when they're available!

Other Agave-Based Spirits

There are three last things you should know: pulque, raicilla, and sotol. These close cousins can often be found at mezcal bars.

Pulque ("PUL-cay") is fermented agave sap (rather than distilled fibers) and is super popular in Mexico.

Raicilla ("RYE-see-ya") is basically mezcal that doesn't fall under the legal definition of mezcal (see page 6). In other words, it's moonshine. Subject to very few regulations, it's usually only distilled once. And since distilling smoothens spirits, raicillas can be pretty funky, and not for the faint of heart!

Finally, sotol ("SO-toll") is a distillate of the sotol plant. Sotol used to be considered part of the *Agave* family, but was reclassified as a *Nolinaceae* instead. Also known as "Dessert Spoon", it is cooked in above-ground clay ovens like tequila and produces a spirit that's clean, fresh, and floral. If you see one on the menu at a mezcalería, be sure to try it out!

What's with the Worm?

Start telling people who are unfamiliar with mezcal that you've fallen in love with it, and inevitably someone will say, "That rotgut booze with the worm in it?!" Yes, mezcal was once known as a cheap liquor popular in Tijuana tourist bars, and it was name-dropped in '60s westerns by badass cowboys who just wanted something strong to get them hammered. As John McEvoy, author of *Holy Smoke! It's Mezcal!* says, the worm set mezcal back fifty years. So what's with the worm and the bad reputation, anyway?

The worm *(gusano)* is actually the larvae of the agave snout weevil or the agave moth, both of which feed on, and do great harm to, agave plants. They began to be added to bottles of mezcal as a marketing gimmick in the '60s. It caught on with tourists, who spread urban legends that the worms imparted hallucinogenic properties into the mezcal. Catering to those who just wanted to chug a bottle of booze and have a wild night out, mezcal companies didn't attend much to quality—as a result, mezcal got a bad reputation that it's still trying to live down.

The worm, however, may have been more than just a way to excite tourists. In his book (a must for any mezcal lover), McEvoy tracks down another theory of the origin of the worm: Some say it was a way for mezcal producers to mark their product as being from Oaxaca rather than Jalisco during the '60s tequila boom.

Regardless of where the worm came from, many mezcal producers would like it abolished all together. Yet you do occasionally run into an artisanal brand (like Wahaka) that includes it as a nod to mezcal's heritage, and as a way of imparting a subtle flavor undertone similar to *sal de gusano* (page 31), a traditional mezcal accompaniment of salt mixed with dried, ground worm.

Sipping Mezcal

The first rule of mezcal is sip it, never shoot it. Although drinking mezcal is about having fun, it's also about respecting the spirit—in every sense of the word "spirit." The agave that created the mezcal you're drinking took at least eight (and up to thirty-five!) years to send up a flower, and was then immediately hacked down,* its life mission complete. *Your* life's mission should be to drink mezcal in the way it's meant to be drunk, straight and slowly—but not too slowly. (Don't worry: Even if you're a novice, we'll show you how—and if you're more of a cocktail person, we've still got plenty of options for you, too!) Whether you're buying a bottle or just sipping mezcal at a restaurant or bar, here's what to look for when deciding what to sample.

---

*Agave plants die a natural death after flowering, so don't feel too sorry for them. However, for more on agave plant sustainability, see page 104.

What to Look for When Choosing a Mezcal

Whether a mezcal newbie or a seasoned sipper, here are important details to look for when deciding what to sample.

Beginner

Is it 100 percent agave?	Any mezcal (including tequila) worth drinking are made from 100 percent agave. Luckily, this is usually displayed prominently on the front of the bottle.
From what varietal of agave is it made?	Most mezcal (that isn't tequila) is made from the espadín varietal of agave. As a beginner, it's usually best to start here—there are a lot of different flavors to explore before you move on to other varietals like tobalá, tobasiche, and arroqueño.
Is it aged?	Most mezcal is unaged or *joven* (young), because agave has so much flavor it doesn't need aging. However, it can be fun to try a *reposado* (rested) or *añejo* (aged) variety.

Is it clear?	All joven mezcal should be clear. Repasado and añejo mezcals will have a bit of a gold tinge.
Is it produced in a small batch?	True mezcal is made in small batches, and while most bottles will tell you the exact size of the batch, as a new mezcal drinker, just be sure to stay away from anything that has a celebrity's name on the bottle or otherwise seems like it might be mass produced.

Advanced

Where was it produced?	Mexican law states that mezcal can only be made in certain states, and each state has its own tradition. Most mezcal producers will even list the village of origin right on their label.
In what type of still is it produced?	Copper and clay stills are both used to produce mezcal, and each lends its own flavor. If you get super adventurous you can even find mezcals made from other types of stills.

What is ABV (alcohol by volume)?	Mezcals range from 40–60 percent alcohol volume. The percentage of alcohol a mezcal is doesn't always dictate how intense mezcals heat and flavor are, so try experimenting!
What special *terroir* contributes to this agave's taste?	*Terroir* describes the environmental factors that can contribute to a spirit's taste, such as climate, amount of sun, and even what's growing nearby.
Which mezcalero made it, and what is his process?	Mezcaleros are the possibly-magical people who make mezcal, usually by a process that has passed down for generations. A bartender who really knows their stuff can often tell you about what makes this particular mezcalero special.
How does this mezcal brand contribute to sustainability efforts? Does it treat its mezcalero and his village in a fair and inclusive way?	This information won't be on the bottle, but is worth trying to find out, usually with some googling. (For more, see page 104.)
Is it infused?	Some mezcals are infused with seasonal fruits, nuts, botanicals, or even raw chicken!) during distillation. (See page 119 for more on these mezcals.)

How to Taste Mezcal

Most likely, the first time you tried straight liquor, all you tasted was its heat—in fact, you were probably just trying to get it down. It was only over a period of months, or perhaps years, that you came to appreciate the subtle flavors and nuances of spirits like gin or scotch.

When people first taste mezcal they typically say "all I taste is the smoke!" or "it's too strong!" Since every person's taste is his or her own, this response can never be wrong, but it's important to give yourself a chance to develop an understanding of what you're drinking. Tastes, after all, reflect memories— a mezcal can't taste "like melon" if you have no memory of eating a melon. Similarly, if all you have to

compare mezcal to is tequila, the first thing that may come to mind is that it's smokier-tasting version of tequila. If mezcal seems too intense at first, remember that you probably once thought the same thing of alcohol in general! Keep sipping, and tasting, and comparing. Soon, you'll move beyond the heat and the smokiness, and then the amazing nuances of mezcal will all open up to you.

What is the Best Vessel for Drinking Mezcal?

You can drink your mezcal out of anything really: a wine glass, an old mug, or a metal flask you keep hidden in your boot. In Oaxaca, and in many American cantinas, you'll see *jícaras*, which are cute little cups made from half a gourd. Strong and sturdy as if hand-carved out of wood, they are containers created by nature itself. Another traditional vessel is a clear votive glass with a cross engraved at the bottom. (You know you're done drinking when you see the sign of the cross.)

Once, while Lindsey was visiting the palenque in San Balthazar Chichicapa, Del Maguey's master mezcalero Faustino García Vásquez poured her some mezcal from a makeshift thermos made out of a Wiffle ball. She drank it from a *copita*, a traditional clay vessel.

No matter what you drink mezcal from, make it something that allows you to experience the mezcal, hopefully by being able to smell its complex aroma before each sip.

Before You Take a Sip

Before you sip the mezcal, begin by looking at it. Is it clear, or can you see a slight color tone? How does it move when it's poured into a glass? You should see bubbles, called perlas (literally "pearls" in Spanish), rising to the top. The most advanced mezcal experts can determine the alcohol by volume (ABV) just by looking at the bubbles! But for now, just notice that they're there and watch what they're doing—bubbles tend to hang around and dance more if there's a higher alcohol content.

Next, smell the mezcal. (This is called its "nose.") A great way to smell the mezcal you're about to taste is to put a drop in your hand, then rub your palms together. This causes the alcohol to evaporate, leaving behind only the scent of cooked agave and other subtle flavor nuances for you to breathe in.

What "smell memories" do you experience? Think about time you've spent outdoors, especially if you've been to Mexico or Central America. Are there flowers blooming, ripe fruit growing, or a dairy farm nearby? Can you smell earth? Fire? All of these aromas can be detected just in the smell of mezcal in your hands. (And if you smell either alcohol or nothing at all—don't waste your time!)

Taking the First (Tiny) Sip

Start off by taking a tiny taste of the mezcal, looking for the undertones you just smelled. Does it taste the same all the way through? If not, what changes about the taste during your sip? Does it taste like it smells? What kind of new flavors can you discern that were different from just smelling it? Does it taste bright, grassy, floral, or citrusy? Some mezcals, like those made with tobalá agave, can even taste salty!

Each Sip

You may be surprised that your second sip tastes different than the first! Keep sipping and taking note of the flavors and memories it evokes. With each sip, gently roll the mezcal around, letting it touch every part of your mouth—especially your taste buds—and notice what kind of body the mezcal has. If the heat of the mezcal is too much to take, make sure to exhale after each sip, then notice what flavors remain.

The dominant flavor characteristics of mezcal come from the taste of the agave itself. Agave is an incredible combination of floral and citrus flavors, even when raw, but the cooking process causes a chemical reaction that releases more undertones which may include hints of nuts, caramel, or vanilla. Some distilleries also add elements to the still to give the mezcal more flavor, like botanicals, dried fruits, corn, or raw chicken. Finally, the fermentation process adds fruity notes like melon or banana. Some—but not most—mezcals are then aged in barrels, which adds an additional woody flavor.

What do you taste as you sip this particular mezcal? Here are some words you might use to describe the experience, but don't be afraid to add your own or even recount a specific memory triggered by the taste.

Roasted red peppers
Peppercorns
Earthy
Clay
Leather
Dark ripe fruits (like raspberry and cherry)
Tropical fruits (like melon and banana)
Citrusy
Dark chocolate
Caramel
Honey
Vanilla
Cotton candy
Floral
Vegetal
Meaty
Bright

Mineral
Wood
Grass
Roasted jalapeños or other green chiles
Nuts
Roasted pumpkin
Mexican herbs (like epazote, hoja santa, or cilantro)
Lemongrass
Salty
Creamy
Hot
Smooth
Complex
Clean
Crisp
Stone

As your sip ends, think about its finish. Again, does it taste different at the end versus the beginning? What kinds of flavors remain? Do you detect any more nuances and undertones as you continue to sip and taste?

Sal de Gusano

If you drink mezcal in Oaxaca, you're likely to do so with some sal de gusano, a salt mixture that includes Mexican chiles and the dried, ground worm (*gusano*) that feeds on agave. (If you're wondering if any mezcal still comes with the worm in the bottle, check out page 19.) While the thought of knowingly eating dried worms may leave you a tad nauseated, the gusano is ground so finely that you can't explicitly taste it—just the hearty "oomph" it adds to the chile and salt. This artisanal salt can be ordered online. Serve *sal de gusano* with orange slices to enjoy between sips of mezcal.

Mixing
Mezcal

Although Ulises Torrentera has famously said that "cocktails are the fanciest manner to degrade mezcal," many other bartenders (and bar patrons) discovered mezcal through cocktails. Since mezcal has undertones of grass, flowers, leather, melon, and a dozen or more other things, it not only goes well with just about every mixer and spirit, but the taste of the mezcal still shines through.

An important point to note is that in our cocktails we only use mezcals from the agave varietal espadín (see page 20). The other varietals are already so flavorful, they should be appreciated unadulterated, especially since batches are small and many agave varietals risk endangerment. We usually make our cocktails with mezcal joven, although a few recipes here call for reposado (aged) mezcal. What brand to use is up to you, but if we have refined a recipe with a particular brand, it's included here as a guide.

The cocktails in the following pages are organized from easy to more complicated. We started with some of the simple classics, like the Mezcal Margarita and a Negroni, and worked our way up to drinks that will have you using some unique ingredients, infusing mezcal with pineapple, making flavored syrups, and more. In addition to the classics (and spins on those classics) we've included some of Lindsey's original drinks as well as cocktails from respected bartenders and other friends in the mezcal world. Feel free to experiment, and have fun! We've included a recommended type of glass and garnish for each drink, but if you don't have them on hand, don't worry. It's more important to use quality ingredients like fresh juice and all-natural spirits.

Mezcal Margarita

Try a mezcal margarita and you'll probably never go back to the tequila-based kind. Use a bright, agave-forward brand like Fidencio Clásico and you don't even need triple sec, which (let's be honest) always brought your homemade margs down a notch.

2 ounces (60 ml) mezcal joven, such as Fidencio Clásico
1 ounce (30 ml) fresh lime juice
½ ounce (15 ml) blue agave nectar or Simple Syrup
(page 42)
Salt, for salting the glass (page 57)
Lime wheel, for garnish

In a cocktail shaker with ice, vigorously shake together all the liquid ingredients until cold and well blended. Strain into a salted rocks glass over ice. Garnish with the lime wheel and serve.

Frozen Margarita

If a frozen margarita is what you want, head to the bar! Bars that serve frozen drinks have special slushie machines that properly mix the ingredients into the ice so you get a drink that's well blended and doesn't get watered down as you drink it. To create that Frozen Marg at home, however, you can use your blender. Use ¼ cup (59 ml) ice for every ounce (30 ml) of liquid you have, and blend it on the highest speed in three-second pulses to help aerate the slush. Drink it down and enjoy!

Oaxacan Negroni

Classically made with gin, Negronis taste equally great (maybe even better) with mezcal.

1 ounce (30 ml) mezcal joven
1 ounce (30 ml) Campari
1 ounce (30 ml) sweet vermouth
Orange peel, for garnish

Pour all the liquid ingredients over ice into a rocks glass and stir until cold and well blended. Garnish with the orange peel and serve.

Última Palabra

A classic Prohibition-era cocktail, The Last Word was also originally made with gin. This version (*Última Palabra* means "last word" in Spanish) has the proportions scaled down to let the mezcal shine through.

1 ounce (30 ml) mezcal joven
¾ ounce (23 ml) green chartreuse
¾ ounce (23 ml) maraschino liqueur, preferably Luxardo
¾ ounce (23 ml) fresh lime juice
Orange peel, for garnish

In a cocktail shaker with ice, vigorously shake together all the ingredients until cold and well blended. Strain into a cocktail glass, garnish with an orange peel, and serve.

Making Your Own Syrups

An essential component in just about every cocktail is added sweetness, and that often comes in the form of syrups, which are just sugar in liquid form. A syrup can be just sugar and water (as in a simple syrup) or it can have other flavors added. Here are a few good syrups to keep on hand to make the cocktails in this book. After letting them cool, store them in the fridge until you're ready to use them.

Simple Syrup

If you've ever been to a coffee shop that offered a clear, sweet liquid to add to your iced coffee instead of granulated sugar, that's simple syrup. And as its name suggests, it's very simple to make. Just add sugar to an equal amount of boiling water, stir to dissolve, then let it cool. It's perfect for adding a touch of sweetness to cocktails (and that iced coffee, too!).

Cinnamon and Canela Syrups

Add a bit of cinnamon to simple syrup and you've got cinnamon syrup! Most cocktail recipes in this book call for canela syrup, which is made from Mexican cinnamon (canela), but a few call for "regular" cinnamon. If you opt for the latter, just know that canela (which you can find in Mexican markets and the international aisle of grocery stores) is a bit sweeter and subtler than the cinnamon you normally find in the spice aisle. You can recognize it by its appearance—it looks more like a peeling bark, almost cigar-like, rather than a firm stick.

To make cinnamon or canela syrup, just add 1 stick canela or ½ stick cinnamon for every ¾ cup (96 g) of sugar you use. Add it to the boiling water while you're dissolving the sugar, and let it sit (covered) for an hour or two before using.

Piloncillo Syrup

Piloncillo is a rich, brown sugar often found in the form of little cones. You can get it at Mexican markets, some grocery stores, and online.

Unlike American brown sugar (which is basically granulated sugar with molasses added to it), piloncillo is minimally processed and comes straight from the sugarcane, giving it all sorts of flavor nuances like dark rum and earthiness.

You can make a cocktail syrup out of piloncillo in the same way you can make simple syrup out of granulated sugar. Just combine equal parts boiling water and piloncillo and stir to combine.

Pomegranate Syrup (aka Grenadine)

Steer clear of grenadine, a pomegranate-flavored, sickly sweet syrup sold at liquor stores and make this rich and interesting sweetener instead. It's easy to do with a bottled pomegranate juice.

16 ounces (250 ml) pomegranate juice
½ cup (64 g) granulated sugar
2 drops fresh lemon juice

Add the ingredients together in a small saucepan and heat them over medium-high heat, stirring occasionally, until the sugar dissolves and the mixture starts to boil. Boil the mixture until it is reduced and drips slowly from the back of a spoon, about 5 minutes.

Zaragoza

This recipe is from bartender Jesús Díaz. Appropriately for the spirit of mezcal, we met Jesús at a bar one night while enjoying some mezcal, and he shared this recipe with us. It's named after the Mexican army general who defeated the French during the Battle of Puebla.

**2 ounces (60 ml) mezcal joven, preferably
Misterios Doba-Yej**
½ ounce (15 ml) Bénédictine
½ ounce (15 ml) Pomegranate Syrup (page 43)
½ ounce (15 ml) fresh lemon juice

In a cocktail shaker with ice, vigorously shake together all the ingredients until cold and well blended. Strain into a coupe or cocktail glass and serve.

El Chupacabra

Based on the vodka-based Greyhound and named after a mythical beast from Latin America, this drink is so super-refreshing that you might even forget about the blood-sucking spiky creature the drink is named for. Unlike with most cocktails, we actually encourage squeezing in some fresh lime juice to taste once it's in the glass.

> **2 ounces (60 ml) mezcal joven**
> **3 ounces (90 ml) fresh grapefruit juice**
> **2 dashes Amargo Vallet Bitters or Angostura**
>   **Aromatic Bitters**
> **1 fresh lime wedge,** for squeezing
> **Lime wedge,** for garnish

In a cocktail shaker with ice, vigorously shake together the mezcal, grapefruit juice, and bitters until cold and well blended. Double-strain into a collins glass over ice. Squeeze in lime juice to taste, and garnish with the additional lime wedge and serve.

Sunset in the Sur

If you've never tried elderflower liqueur, you're about to find a new favorite cocktail ingredient. Often known by its most common brand, St-Germain, it adds a vibrant floral taste that goes wonderfully with any sparkling wine. Here, mezcal and grapefruit juice are added to the mix, which really makes it shine.

> **1½ (45 ml) ounces mezcal joven**
> **¾ ounce (23 ml) elderflower liqueur, preferably**
>   **St-Germain**
> **¼ ounce (8 ml) fresh lime juice**
> **¾ ounce (23 ml) fresh grapefruit juice**
> **Sparkling white wine, such as cava,** for topping
> **Grapefruit peel,** for garnish

In a cocktail shaker with ice, vigorously shake together the mezcal, elderflower liqueur, lime juice, and grapefruit juice until cold and well blended. Double-strain into a coupe glass or flute. Top with the sparkling wine. Garnish with the grapefruit peel and serve.

Lucha Libre

This original cocktail from Harris Tooley complements the mezcal with Spring 44's barrel-aged Old Tom Gin.

1½ ounces (45 ml) mezcal joven, preferably Ilegal
½ ounce (15 ml) Spring 44 Old Tom Gin
1 ounce (30 ml) fresh lemon juice
¾ ounce (23 ml) Simple Syrup (page 42)
2 dashes orange bitters
Soda water, for topping
Dehydrated lemon or lemon twist, for garnish

In a cocktail shaker with ice, vigorously shake together the mezcal, gin, lemon juice, simple syrup, and bitters until cold and well blended. Double-strain into a collins glass over ice. Top with the soda water. Garnish with the dehydrated lemon and serve.

El Martinez

This classic cocktail, most often made with gin, has been called the "missing link" between the Manhattan and the Martini. Instead of using a lemon peel, you can also garnish it with a single maraschino cherry on the bottom of the glass.

> 1 ½ ounces (45 ml) mezcal joven
> 1 ounce (30 ml) sweet vermouth, preferably Dolin
> 2 dashes Amaro Via or Angostura Aromatic Bitters
> 1 barspoon or teaspoon maraschino liqueur,
>   preferably Luxardo
> **Lemon peel,** with or without cherry in center, for garnish

In a mixing glass with ice, stir together the mezcal, vermouth, bitters, and maraschino liqueur until cold and well blended. Strain into a chilled cocktail or coupe glass. Garnish with lemon peel and serve.

Mezcal Martini

Of course you can make a Martini with mezcal! Here's a version with a twist of grapefruit, but any citrus will do.

> 2 ounces (60 ml) mezcal joven, preferably Fidencio
> ½ ounce (15 ml) vermouth blanc, preferably Dolin
> 1 dash grapefruit bitters
> **Grapefruit twist,** for garnish

In a mixing glass with ice, stir together all the liquid ingredients until cold and well blended. Strain into a chilled cocktail glass. Garnish with the grapefruit twist and serve.

Pairing Mezcal with Food

When you drink a Mexican spirit, you want some Mexican food! But not everyone is happy pairing mezcal with meals. "Everybody wants to do these pairing dinners, but I can't stand them," Frontera restaurant owner Rick Bayless tells Emma Janzen in her book *Mezcal*. "You can taste a little mezcal with a dish and say, 'Oh, this goes well' but do you really want to have a whole glass of it with your meal?" Instead, Bayless—like most mezcal experts—prefers his mezcal before a meal, as an aperitif, because it opens up your palate, allowing you to better enjoy your food while not overwhelming it.

Thanks to mezcal's rising popularity, however, some chefs have begun to offer tasting menus with mezcal pairings. They love that mezcal can stand up to strong flavors like steak, smoked meats, and especially spice! If you're enjoying your mezcal with some food, try it with something that compliments the flavors of mezcal, like some chicken mole or fresh, warm tortilla chips with a jar of mango salsa.

In traditional Oaxacan mezcalerías, cacahuates (chile-lime peanuts) and chapulines (cooked and seasoned grasshoppers—yes, grasshoppers) are often served with mezcal served straight up. We've included a chile-lime peanut recipe on page 55, but you're on your own for the grasshoppers (you can buy them online, if you're really curious).

Mezcal is wonderful as a digestif as well. Not only does it help you digest your meal, but it goes perfectly with chocolate. Try it with a chocolate mousse, a dark chocolate bar, or another rich dessert. The mezcal will cut through the intense flavor and make the best part of your meal even better.

Chile-Lime Peanuts

Chile-lime peanuts (cacahuates) are a classic mezcal accompaniment, often found at tastings and cantinas. Here's how to make your own.

- **2 tablespoons (30 ml) fresh lime juice,** plus additional for garnish
- **2 teaspoons (8 g) chile powder**
- **1 teaspoon (4 g) salt**
- **½ teaspoon (2 g) granulated sugar**
- **¼ teaspoon (1 g) cayenne pepper**
- **2 cups (480 g) Spanish peanuts**

Preheat the oven to 250°F (121 C). In a medium bowl, whisk together the 2 tablespoons of lime juice, the chile powder, salt, sugar, and cayenne. Add the peanuts and stir until evenly coated. Pour onto an ungreased baking sheet and bake until the nuts are fragrant and begin to darken, about 30 minutes. Garnish with additional lime juice and eat by the handful.

Ancho Mezcalita

Ancho Reyes Ancho Chile Liqueur is a sublime addition to a mezcal cocktail. Made with dried ancho chiles steeped in a sugarcane-based spirit, it originates in Puebla, one of the newest Mexican states legally allowed to produce mezcal.

1 ounce (30 ml) mezcal joven
1 ounce (30 ml) Ancho Reyes Ancho Chile Liqueur
1 ounce (30 ml) fresh lime juice
½ ounce (15 ml) agave nectar
Chile salt, for garnish (see page 31)
Lime wheel, for garnish

In a cocktail shaker with ice, vigorously shake together all the liquid ingredients until cold and well blended. Salt a rocks glass with a mixture of chile powder (preferably pequin chiles) and salt. Double-strain into the glass over ice and serve.

How to Salt a Glass

Garnishes are supposed to complement your drink—not end up in it. The same goes for salt. Salt the sides of your glass instead of the rim to make sure none falls into your cocktail. Here's how: Get two saucers and pour lime juice in one and salt into the other (Non-iodized, a.k.a. Kosher salt, works best). Dip the side of your glass into the juice, then the salt. Wipe the excess salt off the lip (top) of the glass. Then hold the glass upside down and gently shake it to get rid of the excess salt. Now you're ready to pour your drink.

El Viejo

A classic for a reason, an Old Fashioned has all the elements of a perfect cocktail: the spirit, some sweetness, some bitterness, and a bit of water. This twist, "The Old," adds a bit of spice with Ancho Reyes Ancho Chile Liqueur.

> **1 ounce (30 ml) mezcal joven**
> **1 ounce (30 ml) Ancho Reyes Ancho Chile Liqueur**
> **¼ ounce (8 ml) Simple Syrup** (page 42)
> **2 dashes Regan's Orange Bitters**
> **3 dashes Amargo Vallet Bitters or Angostura Aromatic Bitters**
> **1 thick strip orange peel**
> **1 sprig rosemary,** for garnish

In a mixing glass with ice, stir together the mezcal, chile liqueur, simple syrup, and bitters until cold and well blended. Strain into a rocks glass over one large ice cube. Wipe the orange peel then the rosemary sprig over the lip of the glass. Garnish with the orange peel and serve.

Oaxacan Rosita

This simple, sophisticated cocktail by Charlotte Voisey features Lillet Rosé, a floral rosé liqueur that's worth having in your liquor cabinet because it's also great on its own, straight or on ice.

1 ounce (30 ml) mezcal joven, preferably Montelobos
1 ounce (30 ml) Lillet Rosé
1 ounce (30 ml) Aperol
Orange peel twist, for garnish

In a mixing glass with ice, stir together all the liquid ingredients until cold and well blended. Strain into a cocktail glass. Garnish with the orange peel and serve.

Bitter Bird

Lindsey created this refreshingly bitter drink as a less-sweet twist on a Paloma. Be sure to use a nice, high-quality tonic—look for something in a glass bottle!

> **1½ ounces (45 ml) mezcal joven**
> **1¼ ounces (38 ml) fresh grapefruit juice**
> **½ ounce (15 ml) fresh lime juice**
> **3 dashes Amargo Vallet Bitters or Angostura**
> **   Aromatic Bitters**
> **Tonic water, preferably Q**
> **1 sprig rosemary,** for garnish

In a cocktail shaker with ice, shake together the mezcal, grapefruit juice, lime juice, and bitters until cold and well blended. Strain into a collins glass over ice, top with the tonic, then garnish with the rosemary sprig and serve.

Paloma

A Paloma is a simple, classic tequila drink made with some grapefruit soda, which you probably know by its popular brand name, Squirt.

> **1½ ounces (45 ml) 100% agave tequila**
> **½ ounce (15 ml) fresh lime juice**
> **½ ounce (15 ml) grapefruit soda, such as Squirt**
> **Grapefruit twist,** for garnish

In a cocktail shaker with ice, shake together the tequila and lime juice until cold and well blended. Double-strain into highball glass over ice and top with the grapefruit soda. Stir. Garnish with the grapefruit twist and serve.

Sirena de Muerte

This dark and smoky drink with a touch of balanced bitterness gets a little extra body from Jägermeister and pineapple gum syrup, a gelatin-like ingredient you can buy online. Gum arabic is infused with pineapple for a weightier mixture. This classic ingredient is found in many pre-Prohibition cocktails.

1 ounce (30 ml) mezcal joven
¾ ounce (23 ml) black rum
¾ ounce (23 ml) pineapple gum syrup (see above)
½ ounce (15 ml) Jägermeister
½ ounce (15 ml) Simple Syrup (page 42)
½ ounce (15 ml) fresh lime juice
Seasonal flowers and pineapple leaves, for garnish

In a cocktail shaker with ice, vigorously shake together all the ingredients until cold and well blended. Double-strain into a tiki mug over crushed ice and serve.

Smooth Criminal

Ideal for summer, this simple yet perfect cocktail is by acclaimed bartender Carlos Abeyta.

1½ ounces (45 ml) mezcal joven, preferably Ilegal
½ ounce (15 ml) fresh lime juice
¾ ounce (23 ml) fresh lemon juice
¾ ounce (23 ml) peach purée
Lemon or lime wheel, for garnish

In a cocktail shaker with ice, vigorously shake together all the ingredients until cold and well blended. Double-strain into a rocks glass over ice and serve.

Drinking Mezcal in Oaxaca

Writing about drinking mezcal in Oaxaca is a bit like writing about drinking bourbon in Kentucky—it's an integral part of life. Sipped at both celebrations and memorials, rubbed on rashes, consumed when feeling sick, placed as an offering on Day of the Dead altars, mezcal, in one form or another, has been a part of Mexican culture for hundreds of years.

When visiting Oaxaca, the first thing that may hit as you step outside under the sun is the smell of rich earth combined with other elements from your surroundings—flowers, fruits, and perhaps a whiff of a dairy farm. This is the smell of mezcal. In Oaxacan villages, you'll find mezcal flowing freely, thanks to the village's mezcalero, a figure as common as the local butcher or tailor. To taste a huge variety of mezcals and other agave distillates from around Mexico, head to a mezcalería, or mezcal bar. Inside, for about the equivalent of a dollar (and there's no tipping!), you can get a pour of the mezcal of your choice, often served in a votive glass with a cross on the bottom. The bottle is left at the table for you to look at while you sip, and you're free to enjoy the spirit and the company of your friends without over-attentive waiters. Meanwhile, smoke fills the air and kids pass through selling candy and cigarettes out of wooden boxes. A lot of the mezcal you'll find is made from special palenques (local, custom brewers—sort of like a bar in the US that also brews its own beer). Find something you like and you can usually buy a bottle of it right from the mezcalería you sampled it at! (Just make sure to check with your airline on how many bottles you can bring back.)

Oaxacans don't traditionally drink mezcal in cocktails, but modern mezcalerías and fancy restaurants are starting to embrace the idea more and more. Believe it or not, margaritas made with lime are practically unknown in Oaxaca! More popular mixers are lemon, sour orange, and pineapple juice. For the most part, mezcal is served straight with a bit of sal de gusano (see page 31) on the side. Another popular accompaniment is Sangrita, a drink made with whatever leftover fruit and vegetable juices are available, along with pequin chiles. (see page 94 for how to make your own Sangrita.)

No matter how or where you drink it, mezcal should only be drunk in a spirit of friendship and appreciation. As the saying goes in Oaxaca, "Mezcal is for sacred consumption; all excess is profane."

Mezcal Mule

A "mule" is a drink with ginger in it, and the Mezcal Mule has become much more popular in American craft bars than its predecessor, the Moscow Mule, which contains vodka. Perhaps this is because instead of the flavor blending into the background as vodka often does, mezcal shines through.

> **2 ounces (60 ml) mezcal joven**
> **1 ounce (30 ml) Ginger Juice** (page 120)
> **½ ounce (15 ml) fresh lime juice**
> **½ ounce (15 ml) Piloncillo Syrup or Simple Syrup** (page 43)
> **3 dashes Amargo Vallet Bitters or Angostura**
> **Aromatic Bitters**
> **Soda water,** for topping
> **Mint leaf,** for garnish
> **Candied ginger,** for garnish

Shake vigorously with ice until cold and blended. Double-strain into copper mug over crushed ice. Top with soda. Garnish with mint leaves and candied ginger.

An Easier Mule

Want a Mezcal Mule without all the work? While it won't taste as fresh, you can use ginger beer instead. Find a brand that uses fresh ginger, and make sure it's labeled ginger *beer*, not ginger ale (a remarkably different product for having such a similar name). Pour 2 ounces (60 ml) of mezcal into a glass over ice and then top with ginger beer to taste. Stir gently to mix. Top with a squeeze of lime juice, if desired.

20th Century Boy

Bust out that crème de cacao! This riff on the classic 20th Century comes from La Loba Cantina in Brooklyn and balances the drink's rich undertones with Lillet Blanc and lemon juice. The mezcal has notes of all three. Hit up Trader Joe's or a health-food store for cacao nibs, which are the part of the cacao beans used to make chocolate.

> **1½ ounces (45 ml) mezcal joven**
> **¾ ounce (23 ml) Lillet Blanc**
> **½ ounce (15 ml) fresh lemon juice**
> **¼ ounce (8 ml) light creme de cacao**
> **Cacao nibs,** for garnish

In a cocktail shaker with ice, vigorously shake together all the liquid ingredients until cold and well blended. Double-strain into a chilled coupe glass. Garnish with the cacao nibs or lemon twist— or both—and serve.

La Culebra

Before pouring this original, spirit-forward cocktail, give it one last burst of grapefruit by squeezing a grapefruit peel over the glass, allowing its oils to spritz the sides, then wipe the peel along the inside and outside rim of the glass. Called "expressing" the grapefruit oils, this technique brings the smell of grapefruit right into your nose as you sip, allowing you to use all your senses as you drink.

> 1½ ounces (45 ml) mezcal joven
> ¾ ounce (23 ml) dry vermouth
> ½ ounce (15 ml) John D. Taylor's Velvet Falernum
> 1 full dropper Bittermens Hopped Grapefruit Bitters
>   Grapefruit peel expression
> 1 full dropper Bittermens Hopped Grapefruit Bitters
> 1 wide strip fresh grapefruit peel, for expressing
>   (see above)

In a mixing glass with ice, stir together all the liquid ingredients until cold and well blended. Strain into a chilled rocks glass. Express the grapefruit oils by squeezing the peel over the glass then wipe the peel along the mouth of the glass (discard the peel) and serve.

Manila

This original cocktail by Gabriela Martinez Benecke fuses the Asian flavors of sake (Japanese rice wine) and mandarin oranges with mezcal and maple syrup for a truly special drink. Appropriately, the name "Manila" comes from Manila, Philippines, which was the trade center for Asia and Mexico for about three centuries before the 1800s. Gabriela describes this drink as a less-sweet "grown-up candy," and loves how the sake is able to shine through unmuted.

3 mandarin orange wedges
1 ounce (30 ml) mezcal joven, preferably Ilegal
1½ ounces (45 ml) sake, preferably Junmai
¼ ounce (8 ml) maple syrup
¼ ounce (8 ml) Ginger Juice (page 120)
¼ ounce (8 ml) fresh lemon juice
Mandarin orange twist, for garnish

Muddle the mandarin wedges in a cocktail shaker. Add the remaining liquid ingredients with ice and vigorously shake until cold and well blended. Double-strain into a martini glass. Garnish with the mandarin twist and serve.

Automatic Lover

This drink, created for a Ilegal Mezcal event at their Montauk, New York, surf lodge, is perfect for any summertime pool party.

1½ ounces (45 ml) mezcal joven, preferably Ilegal
¾ ounce (8 ml) pineapple juice
½ ounce (15 ml) Canela Syrup (page 42)
½ ounce (15 ml) fresh lime juice
2 dashes Amargo Vallet Bitters or Angostura
      Aromatic Bitters
Pineapple leaves, for garnish

In a cocktail shaker with ice, vigorously shake together all the ingredients until cold and well blended. Double-strain into a rocks glass over ice.

Nine-Botanical Bramble

Using crushed ice in a drink doesn't just make it look cool, it also turns your drink into an evolving experience. That's because as the ice dilutes the cocktail, the flavor of the drink changes. Additionally, you'll start to smell the garnish more—in this case, basil and blackberry. If you don't have a crushed ice machine, go pick some up at a Sonic. Or put some ice in a bag and smash it with a hammer. This original crushed-ice cocktail showcases Pierdes Alams's +9 Botanical Mezcal, which is infused with juniper berries and other botanicals typically used in making gin.

2 ounces (60 ml) Pierde Almas +9 Botanical Mezcal
¾ ounces (23 ml) crème de mûre (blackberry liqueur)
½ ounce (15 ml) fresh lemon juice
1 barspoon or teaspoon Simple Syrup (page 42)
1-2 fresh blackberries, for garnish
1 basil leaf, for garnish

In a cocktail shaker with ice, shake together all the liquid ingredients until cold and well blended. Double-strain into a snifter over crushed ice. Garnish with the blackberry and basil leaf on a skewer and serve.

How Mezcal Is Made

Agave is a tragic creature. After waiting years—sometimes well over a decade—to grow a flower, it reaches the end of its lifespan and dies. One way to honor this noble plant before it goes? Turn it into mezcal.

A process that's been passed down through generations of Mexicans, making mezcal begins with cutting off the leaves and stalk of a mature agave plant to harvest its piña, the "meat" of the plant. Piñas, as their name might suggest, look somewhat similar to pineapples and (depending on the varietal) can range in size from basketballs to giant, heavy orbs that take three men to roll to the *palenque*, the distillery where the mezcal is made.

Palenques use manpower instead of machinery, favoring artisanal methods developed over hundreds of years rather than modern-day efficiencies. In fact, many palenques have dirt floors and are only just now starting to install basic amenities like electric lights. So by their very nature, palenques produce handcrafted small-batch spirits that, under the watchful eyes of master mezcaleros (mezcal makers), have unique variances in taste and smell.

After the piñas are harvested, either from the palenque's own farm or from the wild, they're roasted in stone pits in the ground, often with the leftover agave leaves right on top. This causes the agave's terpenes, or fats, to release sugars that can be fermented (and turned into mezcal). It also gives mezcal its sweet, ripened-fruit flavor. Once cooked, the piñas are ground to extract their juices either using a stone wheel pulled by a mule or horse or by hand with an instrument called a *canoa y maso*. The agave juice is then placed (usually along with its fibers) in fermentation vats.

Artisanal mezcal is made without adding any yeast during fermentation: the agave breaks down thanks to the microbes it already possesses eating the newly released sugars. What those microbes release is ethanol, that wonderful substance that gets us drunk. (The more terpenes the agave has, the more ethanol is produced.) *Mezcaleros* watch carefully over the agave as it ferments—tasting, smelling, and adding water to the must (as the fermenting mixture called) when necessary.

After a period of three to twelve days (sometimes longer), the must is transferred to copper or steel stills for distillation. Here too the mezcalero's knowledge and skill are critical. He has to know where to "cut" the heated distillate, separating the good from the bad. After the first distillation, the mezcal is distilled a second time—and sometimes a third time. At the mezcalero's discretion, at this stage he can now infuse the mezcal with his own unique flavors like corn, fruit, herbs, or even raw chicken breast. (Read about pechuga mezcal on page 12.) The still is located close to agave undergoing the roasting process, giving the mezcal its characteristic smoky taste.

Although some mezcaleros will then age the occasional batch of mezcal in barrels, most mezcal is drunk as unaged joven mezcal. This is the best way to enjoy the flavors—such as citrus, floral, grass, or vanilla—present in the original, beautiful agave.

El Bandido

This original cocktail from our friend Jen Marshall of Ancho Reyes features their new Verde liqueur. Ancho Reyes Verde is made from bright green poblano peppers and is even spicier than their well-known ancho chile liqueur, which is made with a smoked version of the same pepper. It's also brighter and even herby, and it's a whole new taste experience either with or without mezcal.

1 ounce (30 ml) mezcal joven, preferably Montelobos
1 ounce (30 ml) Ancho Reyes Verde
1 ounce (30 ml) pineapple juice
½ ounce (15 ml) fresh lime juice
½ ounce (15 ml) Simple Syrup (page 42)
Lime wheel, for garnish

In a cocktail shaker with ice, vigorously shake together all the ingredients until cold and well blended. Strain into a rocks glass over ice and serve.

La Catrina

You may know that skeletons are often displayed during Oaxaca's Day of the Dead celebration, but did you know that a political cartoon from the 1910s is partly what made them popular? José Guadalupe Posada's etching La Calavera Catrina (the namesake of this drink) was an image of a skeleton dressed in a rich woman's clothing, meant to satirize Mexican natives who were willing to give up their own traditions as long as they could wear the fancy clothes of their European conquerors.

1 whole ripe strawberry, stemmed
1½ ounces (45 ml) mezcal joven
½ ounce (15 ml) fresh lime juice
½ ounce (15 ml) Pomegranate Syrup (page 43)
3-6 mint leaves, for garnish
Pomegranate seeds, for garnish

Muddle strawberry in a cocktail shaker, then add remaining liquid ingredients and ice. Shake vigorously until cold and blended. Strain into a rocks glass over crushed ice. Garnish with mint leaves and pomegranate seeds and serve.

Bed and Breakfast Man

Had a crazy night out? Bed and Breakfast Man is the perfect "hair of the dog" to help revive you. Although it's always best to salt the side of the glass instead of the rim (see page 57), don't worry about that here: it's nice when a bit of salt falls into the drink while you're climbing back into bed. You can use a lighter beer like Modelo, but Victoria, another Mexican beer, has a bit more body to enjoy with that recovery breakfast.

3 slices cucumber
1 ounce (30 ml) mezcal reposado
½ ounce (15 ml) mezcal joven
1 ounce (30 ml) fresh lime juice
¼ ounce (8 ml) Simple Syrup (page 42)
Pequin chile–salt, for salting the glass (page 57)
Beer, for topping, **preferably Victoria**
Cucumber slices, for garnish

In a cocktail shaker, muddle a cucumber. Add the mezcals, lime juice, simple syrup, and some ice. Vigorously shake the contents until cold and well blended. Salt a pint glass with the chile salt. Double-strain into the glass over ice. Top with beer, garnish with sliced cucumber, and serve.

El Fusilado

This original cocktail by Harris Tooley pairs mezcal with a tawny port and uses cinnamon to complement them both. You can make this drink even better by setting the cinnamon stick garnish on fire then blowing it out; it will burn like a stick of incense. It not only looks impressive, but it brings the smell of the cinnamon into your nose, giving you a fuller experience as you drink.

2 ounces (60 ml) mezcal joven, preferably Ilegal
½ ounce (15 ml) RL Buller Victoria Tawny Port
¼ ounce (8 ml) fresh lime juice
½ ounce (15 ml) Cinnamon Syrup (page 43)
Powdered sugar, for sprinkling
Ground cinnamon, for sprinkling
Star anise, for garnish
Cinnamon stick, for garnish

In a cocktail shaker with ice, vigorously shake together all the liquid ingredients until cold and well blended. Double-strain into a copper mug over crushed ice. Sprinkle with the powdered sugar and ground cinnamon. Garnish with the star anise and a cinnamon stick and serve.

Lost in the Supermarket

Fruit and more fruit! When you're lost in the supermarket, you might as well pick up some produce. This tiki drink showcases mezcal's fruity side. It's worth going online to order the Orange Cream Citrate, which adds a soda jerk–style orange flavor that brings it all together.

1 ounce (30 ml) mezcal joven
1 ounce (30 ml) 100% agave tequila reposado
1 ounce (30 ml) Orgeat Syrup, (page 124) **or Small Hand Foods brand**
½ ounce (15 ml) pineapple juice
½ ounce (15 ml) fresh lime juice
½ ounce (15 ml) fresh lemon juice
1 full dropper Bittermens Orange Cream Citrate
Amargo Vallet Bitters or Angostura Aromatic Bitters
Mint sprigs, for garnish
Dried pineapple, for garnish

In a cocktail shaker with ice, vigorously shake together all the liquid ingredients, except the bitters, until cold and well blended. Double-strain into a tiki mug over crushed ice. Float a few drops of bitters on top. Garnish with lots of fresh mint and serve.

Bloody Maria

There's only one best cocktail for a Sunday morning! Enjoy this mezcal version of the classic Bloody Mary. Use your favorite homemade Bloody Mary mix recipe, or just go for a store-bought mix.

1½ ounces (45 ml) mezcal
2 ounces (60 ml) Bloody Mary mix of your choice
Roasted jalapeños, for garnish
Roasted tomatoes, for garnish
Chile salt, for garnish

In a cocktail shaker with ice, vigorously shake together all the liquid ingredients until cold and well blended. Strain into a rocks glass over ice. Garnish with roasted jalapeño and tomatoes and serve.

Sangrita

Sangrita is a traditional, non-alcoholic drink that's often served alongside mezcal. Because of its red color, many people think it contains tomato juice, like a Bloody Mary (or Maria). However, Sangrita actually gets its color from grenadine. In Mexico, it will often be made with whatever leftover veggies are available. But here's one of our favorite versions, from La Loba Cantina.

1 ounce (30 ml) fresh orange juice
¾ ounce (23 ml) fresh lime juice
½ ounce (15 ml) Pomegranate Syrup (page 43)
1 pinch chile powder, preferably from pasilla chiles

In a cocktail shaker with ice, vigorously shake together all the ingredients until cold and well blended. Strain into a collins glass over ice and serve.

Strange Pursuits

This original is a sweet and spicy cocktail that's full of flavor. It's one of those drinks that just works—all of the individual components come together to make something bigger than the sum of their parts. Just try to serve it without people asking you, "What's in this, anyway?"

2 slices fresh serrano or jalapeño pepper
1 strawberry, stemmed
2 ounces (60 ml) mezcal joven
¾ ounce (23 ml) Orgeat Syrup, (page 124), **or Small Hand Foods brand**
½ ounce (15 ml) fresh lime juice
Jalapeños peppers, for garnish

In a cocktail shaker, muddle the peppers and strawberry. Add the remaining liquid ingredients and some ice. Vigorously shake the contents until cold and well blended. Double-strain into a snifter glass. Garnish with the mint leaves and serve.

Ruby Mayahuel

This drink is our tribute to Mayahuel, the Aztec goddess of maguey (the type of agave grown in Mexico). Known as the goddess of fertility, Mayahuel was said to have four hundred breasts from which she fed her four hundred children (who manifested as rabbits). Legend has it that Mayahuel was killed by her evil grandmother (an even more powerful goddess), and at her burial her lover Quetzalcoatl, the god of redemption, cried tears onto the earth from which the first agave plant grew.

1½ ounces (45 ml) mezcal joven
1 ounce (30 ml) hibiscus tea, cooled
1 ounce (30 ml) ruby port
¼ ounce (8 ml) crème de cacao
Seasonal flowers, for garnish

In a mixing glass with ice, stir together all the ingredients until cold and well blended. Strain into a chilled cocktail or coupe glass and serve.

Kitty Likes Spring

As bonafide cat ladies, we can attest to the fact that kitties like spring—both the season and springy toys. This original cocktail was created as homage to our mutual love of cats and in the spirit of the fun way a kitten freaks out when playing. Like the Ruby Mayahuel, it contains hibiscus tea, a traditional Mexican ingredient.

2 ounces (60 ml) mezcal joven
1 ounce (30 ml) hibiscus tea, cooled
¾ ounce (23 ml) ginger juice (page 120)
½ ounce (15 ml) fresh lime juice

In a cocktail shaker with ice, vigorously shake together all the ingredients until cold and well blended. Double-strain into a collins glass over ice and serve.

Mezcal Sour

Believe it or not, a sour is any cocktail that has a raw egg white in it. It might sound gross, but the egg white gives the drink a fuller mouthfeel and produces a delightful foam on the top. Add the bitters on top of the foam and use a toothpick to create designs for an extra-special presentation. If you don't want to use a raw egg white, you can substitute aquafaba, the juice from a can of garbanzo beans (chickpeas), for an almost identical effect.

> **2 ounces (60 ml) mezcal joven**
> **½ ounce (15 ml) fresh lemon juice**
> **¾ ounce (23 ml) Simple Syrup** (page 42)
> **1 egg white (pasteurized) or 1 ounce aquafaba**
> **(garbanzo bean juice)**
> **2 dashes Amargo Vallet Bitters or Angostura**
> **Aromatic Bitters**

In a cocktail shaker with ice, shake together all the ingredients, except the bitters, for 30 seconds. Add ice and continue to shake until cold, 7 to 10 seconds more. Double-strain into a cocktail or coupe glass. Add the bitters on top of the foam and serve.

Mezcal Sustainability and Cultural Appropriation

If you've started learning more about mezcal, you've mostly likely heard about the sustainability issues the agave plant is facing. With mezcal's popularity skyrocketing (especially in the US), will the plant—especially the varietals that grow in the wild—still be around for future generations to enjoy? Are villages being forced to deplete their own agave reserves for the benefit of their northern neighbors? Are mezcal companies putting profits back into mezcal distilleries, or palenques, while still allowing them to work independently? These questions of sustainability and fairness go hand-in-hand with questions about cultural appropriation, which is when a more advantaged country or culture borrows aspects from another, without understanding the true significance to that culture or caring about the impact of their use.

What happens, and will happen, to Mexicans as mezcal booms in America? As Sarah Bowen puts it in the definitive book on the

subject, *Divided Spirits: Tequila, Mezcal, and the Politics of Production*, "neocolonial evocations of discovery are common" when the media and retailers talk about the origin stories of mezcal brands. In other words, are white Americans discovering mezcal like Columbus discovered America—by taking advantage of indigenous people?

Obviously, it's a complicated subject. Not only is the sustainability of agave a complex issue—over-harvesting agave has even led to a decrease in certain bat populations that pollinates it!—it's one that hasn't been adequately studied. What we do know is that the mezcal industry is one of the most transparent out there, especially when compared to other types of liquors. Unlike other spirits, whose production is driven by industrial factories (some of which have questionable worker conditions—we're looking at you, rum), mezcal is still a handmade product. You can find out the exact name of the person who made it while you sip it; it's usually right on the bottle. Many mezcal brands are working to cultivate formerly wild strains of agave, and working with villages to repopulate their dwindling wild agave stocks.

If you have a favorite brand of mezcal, check out their website or other web presence to see what they're doing to work with palenques, rather than making the palenques work for them. For instance, on Del Maguey's website, you can find out about their wild maguey project to reforest agave. Mezcal Vago goes so in depth into their sustainability efforts that they even talk about the firewood used to roast the agave, the water runoff, and the health impacts on their workers from working with wood-burning stoves. Over on the website Medium, Richard Betts, the owner of Sombra Mezcal, recently wrote a thought-provoking post titled "The Dirty Truth of Making Mezcal and How We Can Do Better," in which he weighs the concerns of "tradition" with those of "environmental impact, sustainability, and ethical considerations."

While these questions aren't easy to answer, at least they're being asked. It appears, unfortunately, that sustainability and appropriation questions are not being asked often enough—or by the right people. In *Divided Spirits,* Bowen concludes that "consumers do not necessarily value social justice, environmental sustainability, or the preservation of cultural traditions," so it has to be up to the government, and not the free market, to impose rules on the manufacturing of mezcal. And in a post for Eater Chicago on the American appropriation of Mexican culture, particularly mezcal, Jay Schroeder (founder of Chicago's Mezcaleria Las Flores), speaks to the importance of mezcal's new devotees realizing their role as observers and teachers, not know-it-alls. He writes:

Mezcal has exploded into the collective consciousness, and rightfully so. Mezcal is delicious. It's the thing the cool kids drink. All self-respecting bartenders either love it or claim to. For me, mezcal represents something deeper. It's a chance to have a very real impact on the lives of actual people. It's a chance to help shape what is already the most unique category in the entire world of spirits, and to do so in a way that preserves a proud set of traditions while economically supporting regions and communities in need. . . At the end of the day, I have to recognize that I am in no way an authority on the subjects I share. At best, I am a conduit of information from the real authorities: Those who produce mezcal and whose lives depend on it.

Oaxaca Earthquake

At midnight on September 8, 2017, an 8.1 magnitude earthquake burst outward from the heart of the State of Oaxaca, where most mezcal originates. Houses, schools and hospitals fell. Power lines collapsed. More than 90 people died. Some reported that two million or more people were left homeless. Thousands of aftershocks finished the devastation as buildings initially damaged now succumbed completely.

Less than two weeks later, a 7.1 magnitude earthquake punished the people in and around Mexico City, as well as the southern states of Puebla, Guerrero and — once again — Oaxaca.

Mexico is one of the most seismically active regions in the world. Its people are familiar with undulating walls and streets that feel like rope bridges. They continue on with daily life, astoundingly unaffected. But the level of ruin created in the space of eleven days in September 2017 is unimaginable to most of us.

The mezcal community responded quickly. Distillers, bars, restaurants, and individuals who simply love this wild spirit all donated, formed funding pages and even traveled to the affected areas to find survivors and help victims. Yet, with all this support, the rebuilding will take years. Your contributions can help facilitate these efforts. There are many organizations working on the ground, but the three largest are Aporta, the Mexican Red Cross, and Fondo Unido Mexico. Visit their websites for details.

Be Nice or Leave

Mezcal is known to spawn magical places, and one of those places is Café No Sé, a mezcal bar in Antigua, Guatemala, said to be the first mezcalería located outside of Mexico. When it all began in 2004, there were very few mezcals approved for exporting, so its owner, John Rexer, ended up coming up with some "creative" ways to get mezcal to Guatemala. Its popularity eventually gave birth to Ilegal Mezcal, one of our favorite mezcals for making cocktails. The name of this cocktail was inspired by Lindsey's visit to Café No Sé and John Rexer's farm, where she saw "Be Nice or Leave" written on a pole outside his house—and it also inspired one of her tattoos!

1½ ounces (45 ml) mezcal joven, preferably Ilegal
**¾ ounce (23 ml) Laphroaig 10-year single malt
   Islay scotch**
½ ounce (15 ml) Honey Syrup (page 131)
3 dashes Dr. Sours #2 Café De Olla
Cacao nibs, for garnish

In a cocktail shaker with ice, vigorously shake together all the liquid ingredients until cold and well blended. Strain into a rocks glass over ice (preferably one large block of ice). Garnish with the cacao nibs and serve.

AC Mezcal

Mezcal is so new on the American bar scene that many craft bartenders are still relatively unfamiliar with it. José María Dondé Rangel is working to change that. He founded the group Panorama Mezcal, which holds events in New York City to help educate bartenders and others about the intricacies of mezcal and the mezcal industry. This mezcal cocktail, which he cr eated, gives you a good use for that ice mold you bought: freezing a cinnamon stick inside it.

> **1¾ ounces (53 ml) mezcal joven, preferably Meteoro**
> **½ ounce (15 ml) Campari**
> **¾ ounce (23 ml) Cinnamon Syrup** (page 43)
> **¾ ounce (23 ml) lemon syrup**
> **Cinnamon stick,** for garnish (see above)

In a cocktail shaker with ice, vigorously shake together all the liquid ingredients until cold and well blended. Double-strain into a rocks glass over an ice block with the cinnamon stick frozen inside and serve.

Lady of Solitude

Named after the patron saint of Oaxaca, this spirit-forward original cocktail with a touch of sweetness is deep and contemplative, like a girl and her drink on a gloomy night.

6 raspberries, plus additional for garnish
1½ ounces (45 ml) mezcal reposado
¾ ounce (23 ml) Campari
¾ ounce (23 ml) fresh lemon juice

In a cocktail shaker, muddle the raspberries. Add the remaining ingredients and ice and shake until cold and blended. Garnish with a raspberry skewer and serve.

I Woke Up Like This

Have you ever had a "dangerous" cocktail? In Jen's book *Dangerous Cocktails: Adventurous Recipes for Serious Drinkers,* she and coauthor Dylan March define them as drinks that are delicious and a tad mysterious—among other things. This cocktail, with its dark color and deep layers of complexity, definitely fits the bill.

> **1 ½ ounces (45 ml) mezcal reposado, preferably Ilegal**
> **¾ ounce (23 ml) Suze liqueur**
> **¾ ounce (23 ml) Borghetti Caffe Espresso Liqueur**
> **3 dashes Bittermens Orange Cream Citrate**
> **1 wide strip lemon peel,** for expressing and garnish

In a mixing glass with ice, stir together all the liquid ingredients until cold and well blended. Strain into a double rocks glass over ice (preferably one large block of ice). Express the lemon oils by squeezing the peel over the glass then wipe the peel along the mouth of the glass. Garnish with the lemon peel and serve.

What's the Best Order?

In what order should you add your cocktail ingredients? The recipes in this book are written in a standard format, beginning with the liquors, then moving on to the mixers. But in the bartending world, drinks are usually built the other way around, with the liquor being added last. Why? Bartenders are taught to start with the smallest, least expensive ingredients first. That way, if they mess up and have to dump out the drink, they're wasting less. It's not a bad way to do your mixing at home either!

Grand Julius

Here's an original twist on a sour that's also technically a fizz (a drink that contains soda water). You'll love the thick consistency of this white, foamy take on a Ramos Fizz. Find orange-flower water (a sweet-yet-floral mixer) at nice liquor stores and supermarkets.

> **2 ounces (60 ml) mezcal joven**
> **½ ounce (15 ml) fresh lime juice**
> **½ ounce (15 ml) fresh lemon juice**
> **½ ounce (15 ml) heavy cream**
> **¾ ounce (23 ml) Simple Syrup** (page 42)
> **1 barspoon or teaspoon orange flower water**
> **1 egg white (pasteurized), or 1 ounce (30 ml) aquafaba (garbanzo bean juice)**
> **Soda water,** for topping

In a cocktail shaker with ice, vigorously shake together all the ingredients except the soda water. (You're supposed to shake a Ramos Fizz for 7 minutes, but we'll let you off with about 30 seconds, just so the cream can get fluffy). Add ice and continue to shake until cold, 7 to 10 seconds more. Double-strain into a collins glass with no ice. Top with the soda water and serve.

A Good Place

This simple-to-make, yet complex-tasting original gets its spiciness from Fernet-Vallet, the Mexican take on amaro.

1 strawberry, plus 1 for garnish
1½ ounces (45 ml) mezcal joven
¼ ounce (8 ml) Fernet-Vallet
½ ounce (15 ml) fresh lime juice
½ ounce (15 ml) Piloncillo Syrup (page 43)
Sliced strawberry, for garnish

Muddle strawberry in cocktail shaker, then add liquid ingredients and ice and shake vigorously until cold and well blended. Double-strain into a coupe glass. Garnish with the strawberry on a skewer and serve.

Why You Should Always Use Fresh Juice

Would you add sour milk to an expensive cup of coffee? If not, then why are you using bottled lime or lemon juice? It's the quickest and easiest way to spoil an otherwise-great cocktail. Not only is it missing the nuanced flavor of its fresh counterpart, but it practically has no flavor at all! Sadly, bottled juice from the supermarket isn't even made with real fruit—it's just a sour chemical and some water in a bottle. Instead of bringing out the flavorful notes of the liquors in your cocktail, it will squash any subtlety they possessed with its bitter-over-everything, take-no-prisoners taste. The one exception? Canned pineapple juice, which can even be better than fresh when pineapple isn't in season.

How to Make Ginger Juice

Ginger juice is a common cocktail ingredient in bars, and it's not that hard to make at home. Even if you only use a splash of it in your cocktails, your friends will flip for the aggressively fresh and zesty taste it adds to drinks.

½ pound (225 g) fresh ginger, peeled and roughly chopped
1 cup (250 ml) water
2 tablespoons (30 g) granulated sugar

Place the ginger, water, and sugar in a blender and blend until well combined. Strain through a cheesecloth, squeezing to capture all the juice. Strain the juice once more before storing in the refrigerator in a sealed (preferably glass) container.

You don't even have to have a juicer to make juice. Before halving a lime or lemon, roll it back and forth on the counter under your palm, which will release some of the juice before you cut it. Squeeze the juice through a fine-mesh strainer or cheesecloth to catch the seeds and pulp. If you get sick of squeezing, try using a fork or a beater from an electric mixer: place the citrus half in the palm of one hand, hold the beater in the other, and twist it back and forth. Or use a pair of tongs to squeeze each citrus half. Keep unused lemons and limes in a bowl of water in your fridge and they'll last for a month or two. Still seems like a pain? Do it anyway! Your drinks—and your guests—will thank you.

Infused Mezcal

Infusing herbs, chiles, or fruit into mezcal is a fantastic way to add flavor to your cocktails or to just give yourself an interesting sipping experience. It's pretty easy, too. To make an herb-infused mezcal, take a sprig (or about 5 leaves) of fresh herbs and add them to the mezcal. For a fruit-infused mezcal, use about a cup of cubed fruit. For the *Almost Famous* (page 132), for example, Jordan Brower recommends using about ¾ of a pineapple minus the core or "heart"). Let it sit for 3 days. For chiles, you'll have to decide for yourself how hot you want it—start with one or

 two peppers and work your way up. Also, you'll only have to let it infuse for about 24 hours to get the kick you need. (And for any fruit- or chile-infused mezcal, strain it afterwards to remove the bits of fruit or chile.) Finally, if you'd like to infuse your mezcal with marijuana (yes, that's a thing), do some googling on indica or sativa flowers infused in mezcal. That's it!

Santo Domingo

This densely layered drink is perfect for a stormy night. The crème de cassis (blackcurrant liqueur), herby green chartreuse, and fruit juices combine to give this original cocktail a taste reminiscent of blackberries.

1½ ounces (45 ml) mezcal joven
½ ounce (15 ml) crème de cassis
¼ ounce (8 ml) Green Chartreuse
½ ounce (15 ml) pineapple juice
¾ ounce (23 ml) fresh lime juice
½ ounce (15 ml) Piloncillo Syrup (page 43)
Banana leaf and string, for serving

In a cocktail shaker with ice, vigorously shake together all the liquid ingredients until cold and well blended. Double-strain into a rocks glass over ice. Wrap the glass with a banana leaf to make it extra pretty and serve.

Tigre

Here's another original from José María Dondé Rangel. This one contains a homemade sunflower-orgeat syrup.

1½ ounces (45 ml) mezcal joven, preferably Marca Negra
½ ounce (15 ml) 100% agave tequila reposado
¾ ounce (23 ml) Sunflower-Orgeat Syrup (see below)
¾ ounce (23 ml) fresh lime juice
Lemon peel, for garnish

Shake vigorously with ice until cold and blended. Double-strain into a chilled coupe glass and serve.

Homemade Sunflower-Orgeat Syrup
Orgeat syrup is made from almonds and we're adding sunflower seeds.

1½ cups (360 g) raw shelled sunflower seeds
½ cup (120 g) raw, sliced almonds
1½ cups (360 g) granulated sugar
2 dashes orange-flower water
1 ounce (30 ml) vodka

Place the sunflower seeds and almonds in a bowl and cover with water. Let them soak for 20 to 30 minutes, then strain through cheesecloth and discard the water. In a medium saucepan, combine the sunflower-almonds, sugar, and 1¼ cups (160 g) water. Stir continuously over low heat until the sugar dissolves. Remove from the heat and add the orange flower-water and vodka (as a preservative). Refrigerate at least 3 to 4 hours or overnight. Strain out the almonds and sunflower seeds using cheesecloth. Store the syrup in the refrigerator.

Vegan in Spurs

This original sour drink gets its name from the aquafaba used instead of the traditional egg white. Aquafaba is a fancy name for the liquid that comes out of a garbanzo bean (chickpea) can and is perfect for getting a nice foam in your drink, so your friends who don't consume animal products will appreciate you even more!

1½ ounces (45 ml) mezcal joven
¼ ounce (8 ml) Cynar
1 ounce (30 ml) aquafaba
½ ounce (15 ml) fresh lemon juice
¾ ounce (23 ml) Canela Syrup (page 42)
½ dropper Bittermens Hopped Grapefruit Bitters
Freshly grated canela (cinnamon), for garnish

In a cocktail shaker without ice, shake together all the liquid ingredients for 30 seconds. Add ice and shake until cold, 7 to 10 seconds more. Double-strain into a cocktail or coupe glass. Garnish with the canela and serve.

Cinco de Quatro

Here's another original drink—this one by Dylan March—that features Ancho Reyes Verde. In this spirit-forward cocktail, he complements the Verde and mezcal with sublime Banane du Brésil (banana liqueur) and mole bitters, both of which are a great addition to your mezcal cocktail arsenal.

> **2 ounces (60 ml) mezcal joven, preferably Ilegal**
> **½ ounce (15 ml) Ancho Reyes Verde**
> **½ ounce (15 ml) Giffard Banane du Brésil liqueur**
> **3 dashes Bittermens Xocolatl Mole Bitters**
> **1 wide strip fresh lemon peel, for expressing**
> **Dried banana chip,** for garnish

In a mixing glass with ice, stir together all the liquid ingredients until cold and well blended. Strain into a double rocks glass over ice (preferably one large block of ice). Express the lemon oils by squeezing the peel over the glass then wipe the peel along the mouth of the glass (discard the peel). Garnish with the banana chip and serve.

Bat's Knees

Created with the classic Bee's Knees in mind, this version, using sage-infused mezcal is better than the original. Although Bee's Knees got its name from the use of honey, hers gets its name from the animal that pollinates agave: bats!

¼ ounce (8 ml) raw honey
1½ ounces (45 ml) sage-infused mezcal (see page 121)
½ ounce (15 ml) fresh lemon juice
¼ ounce (8 ml) warm water
Sparkling white wine
Sage leaf and lemon twist, for garnish

Stir the honey into warm water until it's smooth. Refrigerate until slightly cooled. Add the honey syrup to a cocktail shaker with ice. Add the lemon juice and mezcal and shake vigorously until cold and well blended. Double-strain into a stemmed glass. Top with the sparkling wine and the sage leaf wrapped in the lemon twist and serve.

Almost Famous

Here's another drink that features infused mezcal, this time a pineapple-infused Sombra that might inspire you to create a cocktail of your own. This sophisticated take on the Naked and Famous is by Jordan Brower of the legendary New York mezcalería Mayahuel.

1 ounce (30 ml) Pineapple-Infused Mezcal
(see page 121), **preferably made with Sombra**
1 ounce (30 ml) Yellow Chartreuse
1 ounce (30 ml) Aperol
1 ounce (30 ml) fresh lemon juice
1 barspoon or teaspoon Honey Syrup (see page 131)

In a cocktail shaker with ice, vigorously shake together all the ingredients until cold and well blended. Double-strain into a coupe glass and serve.

Naked and Famous

The Almost Famous is a more complex take on a Naked and Famous, one of the first "classic" mezcal cocktails, by Joaquin Simó of the immortal cocktail bar Death & Company. If you don't have time to infuse mezcal with pineapple (frowny face), try this original instead.

¾ ounce (23 ml) mezcal joven
¾ ounce (23 ml) Yellow Chartreuse
¾ ounce (23 ml) Aperol
¾ ounce (23 ml) fresh lime juice

In a cocktail shaker with ice, vigorously shake together all the ingredients until cold and well blended. Double-strain into a coupe glass and serve.

Mexican Milk Punch

Milk punches are wonderful with desserts and to serve at parties. Enjoy them especially during Mardi Gras as they are a New Orleans tradition. Naturally, we had to kick up milk punch with mezcal for this take on a classic.

> **1½ ounces (45 ml) mezcal joven**
> **½ ounce (15 ml) black rum**
> **4 ounces (125 ml) milk**
> **1 ounce (30 ml) heavy cream**
> **½ ounce (15 ml) Piloncillo Syrup** (page 43)
> **1 barspoon or teaspoon vanilla extract,**
>   **preferably Mexican vanilla**
> **Freshly grated nutmeg or canela (cinnamon),** for garnish

In a cocktail shaker with ice, briefly shake together all the liquid ingredients until cold and well blended (be careful not to shake too long to avoid diluting the drink). Strain into a mug and garnish with the nutmeg and serve.

La Loba's Agua Fresca

This coconut horchata–based drink comes from Montelobos Mezcal's Camille Austin aka La Loba ("The Wolf"). Horchata is a traditional Mexican drink that's a bit similar to rice pudding, except it's soaked instead of cooked and the rice is strained out. You can find it at many independently run Mexican restaurants—pop in and ask them if they have coconut horchata and use it to make this delicious cocktail, or make your own by replacing regular milk with canned coconut milk in your favorite hourchata recipe.

> 1¼ ounces (38 ml) mezcal joven, preferably Montelobos
> ¾ ounce (23 ml) Ancho Reyes Ancho Chile Liqueur
> ½ ounce (15 ml) Giffard Banane du Brésil liqueur
> ½ ounce (15 ml) Orgeat Syrup, (page 124), or Small Hand Foods brand
> 5 ounces (150 ml) coconut horchata
> Orchid, for garnish
> Orange slice, for garnish
> Freshly grated nutmeg, for garnish

Combine all the liquid ingredients in a highball glass with some crushed ice and stir lightly. Add more ice and a striped-paper tiki straw. Garnish with the orchid, orange slice, and nutmeg and serve.

Types of Cocktail Glasses

Which glass is which? While you don't have to pour the cocktails in this book into the recommended glasses, it can be fun to build up your home collection with a full set of barware. If you're not sure what you've got in your cabinet, here's a quick reference.

Pint

Flute

Collins

Martini

Nick & Nora

Rocks (a.k.a. Old-Fashioned)

Snifter

Copper Mug

Cocktail

Types of Barware

Like all professions, mixologists require specialized tools. How much you choose to invest in your home barward depends completely on your preferences and budget.

For the recipes in this book, the following items are helpful. Those deemed "essential" are marked with a diamond (♦).

♦ **Jigger** - Typically the larger cup on this hourglass-shaped tool measures 1½ ounces (45 ml) while the smaller cup measures ¾ ounce (23 ml). Be careful to confirm these proportions, however, as some jiggers vary in size.

♦ **Measuring Cup** - For measuring fruit juices and other ingredients Measuring Cup - For measuring fruit juices and other ingredients.

♦ **Cocktail Shaker**

♦ **Cocktail Strainer** - Holds back the ice when pouring a drink from your shaker.

♦ **Mesh Strainer** - Many of these recipes require double-straining. The process is actually quite simple: a cocktail strainer fits inside your cocktail shaker, and the contents of shaker are poured through a second, mesh strainer into the glass. The combination of two strainers prevents both ice and pulp and leaves from entering your cocktail.

♦ **Barspoon** - Choose one at least 12" (30 cm) long.

♦ **Cocktail Skewers** - For presenting garnish in the glass, or on the rim.

♦ **Muddler** - Can be stainless steel or wood. The former lasts longer and offers the added benefit of being used to crush ice.

Grater - To create garnishes such as shaved chocolate or grated cinnamon.

Garnish Peeler - This should be a bar-dedicated tool, not the same one you use to peel potatoes or red beets.

Clean Bar Towels - You can buy an electric ice crusher if you choose, but the easiest way to crush ice is to wrap the cubes in a clean towel and give them a solid whack.

Ready, Fire, Aim

Mezcal cocktails are relatively new, but this one by Steve Schneider is already a modern classic. You can find Bittermens Hellfire Habanero Shrub (a hot sauce made specifically for cocktails) online. Use it to experiment with your own cocktails.

> **1 ¾ ounces (53 ml) mezcal joven**
> **1 ounce (30 ml) Honey-Pineapple Syrup** (see below)
> **¾ ounce (23 ml) pineapple juice**
> **½ ounce (15 ml) fresh lime juice**
> **3 dashes Bittermens Hellfire Habanero Shrub**
> **Freshly ground pink peppercorn,** for garnish

In a cocktail shaker with ice, vigorously shake together all the liquid ingredients until cold and well blended. Double-strain into a chilled cocktail glass. Garnish with a grind of fresh pink peppercorn and serve.

Honey-Pineapple Syrup

The not-so-secret-anymore ingredient in this mezcal classic is Honey-Pineapple Syrup, a sweetener you'll want to accidentally dribble on yourself so you can lick it off your fingers. It's crazy delicious and simple to make.

> **½ fresh pineapple** (core removed), cubed
> **1 cup (250 ml) raw honey**
> **1 cup (250 ml) warm water**

Place the pineapple in a glass pitcher or large bowl. Stir the honey and warm water together until smooth, then stir the mixture into the pineapple. Let sit for at least 4 and up to 12 hours, then strain. Store the syrup in a sealed glass container in the fridge.

Taco Truck

Kümmel, a liqueur with overtones of cumin and caraway, gives this original drink its spicy taste and its name, since it tastes vaguely like a one of those ground beef tacos you used to love as a kid.

1½ ounces (45 ml) mezcal joven
¾ ounce (23 ml) dry vermouth
¾ ounce (23 ml) Kümmel liqueur
1 full dropper Bittermens Hellfire Habanero Shrub
Epazote leaf or cilantro sprig, for garnish

In a mixing glass with ice, stir together all the liquid ingredients until cold and well blended. Strain into a cocktail or coupe glass. Garnish with the epazote leaf.

Heels in the Ground

This original drink from Brian Evans of New York's Santina calls for a rinse and a mist. To rinse a glass, roll the liqueur (in this case, allspice dram) around the glass, then discard the excess before pouring the drink in. Then use a stainless-steel or glass atomizer to create the mist. This adds not only a bit of the allspice dram flavor, but its scent as well.

1¼ ounces (45 ml) mezcal joven, preferably Del Maguey Vida
¾ ounce (23 ml) 100% agave tequila reposado
¼ ounce (8 ml) pear brandy, preferably St. George
¾ ounce (23 ml) fresh lemon juice
½ ounce (15 ml) Cinnamon Syrup (page 43)
1 dash absinthe, preferably St. George
Allspice dram, for rinse and mist
Lemon wheel, for garnish

In a cocktail shaker with ice, vigorously shake together all the liquid ingredients, except the allspice dram, until cold and well blended. Rinse a coupe glass with the allspice dram (see headnote). Double-strain into the glass and mist (see headnote) with additional allspice dram. Garnish with the lemon wheel and serve.

Six Shooter

Here's another truly original drink by Jordan Brower. Inspired by a cocktail called the Revolver (an Old Fashioned with coffee liqueur), but with a Manhattan spin, it has exactly six ingredients. After firing a six shooter will smoke, so smoky mezcal makes a perfect base for this drink in more ways than one.

1 ounce (30 ml) mezcal joven, preferably Del Maguey Vida
½ ounce (15 ml) El Dorado 12-Year Rum
½ ounce (15 ml) Smith & Cross Jamaican Rum
½ ounce (15 ml) Amaro Ramazzotti
½ ounce (15 ml) Punt e Mes
1 barspoon or teaspoon Coffee-Demerara Syrup
    (see below)
1 dash Angostura Aromatic Bitters
1 dash orange bitters

In a mixing glass with ice, stir together all the ingredients until cold and well blended. Strain into a Nick & Nora glass and serve.

To-Die-For Coffee-Demerara Syrup

The secret to Jordan's impressive cocktail is Coffee-Demerara Syrup. To make the syrup, simply combine cold-brew coffee with demerara sugar in a 2-to-1 ratio (½ cup coffee (120 g) and ¼ cup (60 g) sugar). Add together and blend until smooth. Cold-brew coffee can be found at big supermarkets and natural food stores (Jared prefers Stumptown brand from Portland). Demerara is a kind of sugar that can be found in the baking aisle of your grocery store—if not, try online.

Me + Julio

This original cocktail by Meredith Sheehy of La Loba Cantina uses freshly grated canela (cinnamon) on top, allowing you to fully engage your sense of smell to really bring out the flavor—leave it on top of the foam (don't mix it in!) and use a swizzle stick to hold back the ice so you can smell as you sip.

> **¾ ounce (23 ml) mezcal joven**
> **¾ ounce (23 ml) 100% agave tequila**
> **1½ ounces (45 ml) tamarind purée**
> **½ ounce (15 ml) Canela Syrup** (page 42)
> **½ ounce (15 ml) fresh lime juice**
> **Freshly grated canela (cinnamon),** for garnish

In a cocktail shaker with ice, vigorously shake together all the liquid ingredients until cold and well blended. Strain into a rocks glass over ice. Grate the canela over the foam and serve.

Dos Diablitos

This is a fun double shot created one night at La Loba Cantina as a way of bringing people together. Bars serve as a community table—a place to make friends and to meet your neighbors. Thus, this cocktail is served in two shot glasses, so you either have to share it with a friend, make a new friend, or decide to be selfish with the two drinks in front of you. In our experience, most people choose to make a new friend—always a great choice. Salud!

½ ounce (15 ml) mezcal joven
¾ ounce (23 ml) crème de cassis
¾ ounce (23 ml) Ginger Juice (page 120)
½ ounce (15 ml) fresh lime juice
½ ounce (15 ml) Piloncillo Syrup (page 43)

In a cocktail shaker with ice, vigorously shake together all the ingredients until cold and well blended. Double-strain into two votive glasses. Share with an old or new frien

Further Reading

Bowen, Sarah. *Divided Spirits: Tequila, Mezcal, and the Politics of Production.* Berkeley: University of California Press, 2015. If you're truly a mezcal nerd, check out this scholarly yet readable book, which argues that mezcal industry must "move beyond market-based models if we want to safeguard local products and the people who make them." Not only does Bowen include bibliographical sources too numerous to count, but she also talks to mezcalaros and distilleries themselves to assess what effect the booming mezcal industry has on them, the local economy, and the future sustainability of the agave plant.

Coss, Susan, and Max Garrone. Mezcalistas.com. If you love mezcal, visit this website right now! It lists the best mezcal bars all around the US and the world, hosts tastings, and has pretty much everything else you need to know about mezcal—from blog posts on Oaxacan customs to tasting notes on the various mezcal brands.

Goodyear, Dana. "The Mezcal Tour of Oaxaca," *The New Yorker,* April 4, 2016. (Available at newyorker.com/magazine/2016/04/04/the-mezcal-tour-of-oaxaca) The New Yorker traces the origins of the recent mezcal boom in the US.

Janzen, Emma. *Mezcal: The History, Craft & Cocktails of the World's Ultimate Artisanal Spirit.* Minneapolis: Voyageur Press, 2017. Like an episode of an Anthony Bourdain show all about mezcal, but in book form, this guide by drinks writer Janzen is packed with plenty of quotes from experts and some recipes for tasty cocktails, too.

McEvoy, John. *Holy Smoke! It's Mezcal! A Complete Guide from Agave to Zapotec.* Mezcal PhD Publishing, 2014. A must-read for anyone who loves mezcal and wants to know everything about it, this comprehensive guide includes information about how mezcal is produced, its history and how it became so popular, controversies about industry practices, and more. It also contains tasting notes on just about every brand, extensive notes about different varietals of agave, and even some easy cocktail recipes. McEvoy also has one of the best websites about mezcal out there: MezcalPhD.com.

Panorama Mezcal. Facebook.com/PanoramaMezcal. A great resource for recent news about mezcal, this group of mezcal enthusiasts also holds fantastic mezcal events in New York City aimed at introducing bartenders and others to this amazing spirit.

Saldaña Oyarzábal, Ivan. *The Anatomy of Mezcal.* **New Jersey: ExpressIt Media, 2013. Translated by María Álvarez.** Like many mezcals, this book can be hard to find. But if you're interested in a fun and extremely readable tutorial on how mezcal is made, Saldaña's tome couldn't be more perfect. The founder of Montelobos Mezcal, Saldaña has a PhD in biochemistry and he covers the history of agave, explains how mezcal gets its flavor, and offers an in-depth look at the process of making mezcal. The engaging design, beautiful agave illustrations, and other touches make it a joy to flip the pages and find out more.

Schroeder, Jay. "I'd Rather Not Celebrate Cinco de Mayo Than Be Part of Cultural Appropriation," *Eater Chicago,* **May 5, 2017.** (Available at chicago. eater.com/2017/5/5/15562344/cinco-de-mayo-chicago-jay-schroeder-mezcal-cultural-appropriation-mexico) One of Chicago's best-known ambassadors of mezcal (who's also studied sociology) discusses his concerns about the American appropriation of Mexican traditions, including mezcal. He includes a checklist of questions to ask yourself about your own cultural appropriation.

Torrentera, Ulises. *Mezcalaria: The Cult of Mezcal.* **Translated by John Dicky. Oaxaca, Mexico: Farolito Ediciones, 2012 (bilingual edition).** One of the grandfathers of mezcal, Torrentera is a mezcal purist through-and-through. In Mezcalaria, he not only does a thorough and thoughtful examination of the history (and future) of mezcal and agave, but he also writes some of the most lyrical passages published about the love of this spirit. Translated into English with the Spanish version printed next to it, this book can be hard to find but deserves a prominent place in your mezcal library.

Photo Credits

All photography unless otherwise noted:
© 2017 Mark A. Gore, mag_foto2mac.com

© Angeliki Jackson, pp: 1, 2-3, 6, 35; © Herminio Torres, pp: endpapers, ii, iii, 68-69, 82, 104;

Shutterstock: p 5: © Sam Carrera; p 11: © aaor2550; p 15: © Chris Curtis; p 19: © Triff;
p 27: © Stefano Spicca; p 28: © jumpingsack; p 42: © lidante; p 43: © FX Media Nagercoil;
p 104: © Jose de Jesus Churion Del; p 121: © JM Travel Photography;
p 138: Africa Studio, Copper: © Danny Smythe; p 138: © Stockcreations.

p 16: Detroit Publishing Company Collection, Prints & Photography Division,
Library of Congress, LC-D4-3914

p 161 © iStock/dia de la muerta

With kind appreciation and Salud! to Meredith and Jeff of La Loba Cantina for their generosity
and wonderful spirit. Visit them and say hello. http://lalobacantina.com

Extending a hearty thank you to Warehouse Wines and Spirits, NYC, for their generous support.
https://www.warehousewinesandspirits.com

Many thanks to Zach Townsend Editorial Services and very special thanks to Stephanie Hoover
for her editorial expertise.

Never drink and drive; always designate a driver.